I like and admire Ho Peng Kee. He has made several important contributions to Singapore: in legal education and in government. He is a leader with integrity and compassion.

Professor Tommy Koh
Ambassador-At-Large, Ministry of Foreign Affairs

People are obviously very important to A/P Ho Peng Kee. This comes out in the way the subtitle *Practical Lessons in Leadership*, is developed in his book, *My Journey in Politics*. His recollection of events, and what he did, are invariably framed by the people he has been involved with. A/P Ho does not espouse trite political or management principles, but rather relies on experiences and interactions with the people he has met in the university, in the hall of residence, as a church elder, in politics, and as a leader of constituency activities and MinLaw initiatives.

Boundless enthusiasm and help for good causes proposed by students, friends and colleagues has been the defining approach of A/P Ho; in my case, in his support in the early days of the Law Awareness projects, which have continued from strength to strength for over 20 years.

N. Sreenivasan SC
Managing Director, Straits Law Practice LLC, and
Former "Block-Head", Kent Ridge Hall, National University of Singapore

My Journey in Politics is a frank story and journey of a Singaporean who became a Minister in two significant Ministries, Law and Home Affairs, contributing to the greater good of the nation. It fits well into the historical tapestry and narrative of Singapore's journey to a first world nation, with fastidious respect for the rule of law and justice, and law and order. Ho Peng Kee's must read maiden speech defines his approach to politics: for Singaporeans to be affirming and encouraging of one another. For Peng Kee, this trait is spontaneous and noetic.

It propels him to come alongside his constituents, lifts up and impacts people and organisations, and humanises tough policies.

Yet *My Journey in Politics* shows Peng Kee's resilient inner man and overcoming leadership through many twists and turns in robust politics. His account of the 2001 general elections in his Nee Soon East SMC is gripped with high drama.

After 20 years of fulfilling and distinguished service to the cause of Singapore, he voluntarily seeks a respite from political life to walk another mile, that of serving God and finishing well.

Citizen, Harvard scholar, Law Professor, Member of Parliament, debater, leader, grassroots man, Minister, peacemaker, patron of charities, Christian disciple: *My Journey in Politics* is summa cum laude!

Richard Magnus
Former Senior District Judge;
Chairman, Public Transport Council; and
Chairman, Temasek Foundation Cares

My Journey in Politics succinctly captures the contributions Peng Kee made to Singapore in his two decades of public service as a Member of Parliament and a Minister of State. In his characteristically frank and direct manner, he described his practical, hands-on experiences in the various and many roles assigned to him. He was deeply involved in helping to formulate and implement policies of the Ministries of Home Affairs and Ministry of Law which have a significant impact on the lives of Singaporeans. He was as passionate in showing his concern for vulnerable groups — like youth at risk, drug addicts, physically assaulted wives, ex-offenders, special needs children, mental health patients — as he was in promoting healthy lifestyle activities like brisk walking, football, or community causes like children's cancer. He distilled the lessons learnt into a "Lessons in Leadership" section at the end of each chapter. These are useful summaries of his experiences which readers will find interesting.

Even after his retirement from active politics, Peng Kee is still serving as a volunteer and promoting causes close to his heart, in the Ministry of Home Affairs' Home Team Volunteer Network Steering Committee, and the Ministry of Law's Advisory Committee on Community Mediation.

Wong Kan Seng
Former Deputy Prime Minister/Minister for Home Affairs

I first met Ho Peng Kee when he entered Parliament in 1991. He was quietly effective and knew his subject matter well. His speeches were a delight to listen to. They were clear, cogent, and concise.

In 2001, Peng Kee, as PAP Second Organising Secretary, asked me to take on the post of Executive Director of Party HQ and PCF HQ. We worked closely together. His leadership style was to outline key objectives of projects assigned to us but left it to us to complete the task. Occasionally, when we did not do as well as expected, he did not have harsh words for us but reminded us that he had trusted us and we should do better. When we implemented a new system of submitting operational reports to HQ, Peng Kee fine-tuned the framework for implementation. Appreciating ground concerns, he then took pains to explain to those affected the purpose and intent of the exercise which they appreciated.

Peng Kee's empathy and compassion for others was clear to all who knew him. He treated everyone with the same kindness and concern. When a staff member ran into financial difficulties, he offered to help her tide over the difficulty without any hesitation.

It was a rewarding nine years for me working with Ho Peng Kee. I learnt from him not only how to look at the big picture and get the priorities right but also the important values of trust, empathy, compassion and respect for others, regardless of their position.

Lau Ping Sum
Former MP/Executive Director, PAP HQ and PCF HQ

I worked with Ho Peng Kee in several key areas viz as Chairman of the Committee on Sporting Singapore (COSS), as Minister for Community Development, Youth and Sports, and as Speaker of

Parliament. In my regular interactions with Peng Kee, I had always found him sincere and upfront. In our working relationship, I found him dependable, enthusiastic and energetic in whatever tasks he was handling. He knew his subject matter well, was always a team player, and a pleasant colleague to work with.

Abdullah Tarmugi
Former Speaker of Parliament/
Minister for Community Development, Youth and Sports

Candid. Intimate. Passionate. Compassionate. Peng Kee reflects on his life as a politician and shares personal leadership principles gleaned from this journey. A must-read for anyone interested in politics and leadership.

John Ng
Chief Passionary Officer, Meta Consulting; and
author of several books on leadership

Associate Prof Ho is a passionate builder of consensus for team actions. He knows his "grounds" well. He also has consummate patience and the ability to bring potentially different mindsets on board with him.

This "ground commander" talent was amply manifested by Prof Ho's significant contributions at all levels at the Ministry of Home Affairs during conceptualisation, planning, and the implementation of the Ministry's far-reaching Drug Rehabilitation initiatives since the early 1990s.

Kong Mun Kwong
Member, Home Team Volunteer Network Steering Committee; and
longstanding grassroots leader and volunteer

Children growing up in Yishun remember Professor Ho Peng Kee well. Known to us as "Uncle Ho" or "Professor Ho", his is a familiar face, welcomed by residents in our neighbourhoods. His down-to-earth, easy-going, and unassuming personality earned him the admiration and respect of many younger residents. Many appreciated his effort in trying to remember our names.

In my late 20s and a Nurse Manager now, I was fortunate to grow up under his leadership. His guidance and mentoring had a great impact on young residents like myself, shaping me into what I am today. I have embraced his natural motivation to serve the community as I take on grassroots leadership positions to promote community bonding.

Till today, his appearance in the constituency still attracts a lot of attention as residents eagerly greet and meet him. For me, speaking to Prof Ho on various occasions seemed like I was sharing with a relative who has seen me grow up over the years. Such is the intimacy he enjoys with Nee Soon East residents.

Yvonne Yap
Vice-Chair, Women's Executive Committee,
Nee Soon East Community Club

I have known Peng Kee for a long time. He is a true friend. As a person, he is cheerful and comfortable under his own skin. He puts people at ease and draws them to him by his openness and sincerity. When deciding on a course of action, he incorporates what is best in other people's contributions to fashion outcomes that are well-judged. His decisions are guided by sound moral principles delivered in a way which respects diversity. When he disagrees, he takes time to ensure that feelings are not hurt. Peng Kee goes out of his way to assist people. As a leader, he is quick to recognise talent and leaves room for people to excel. Our community needs more people like him.

John Ang
Senior Fellow, Social Work Department,
National University of Singapore, and
Former Kent Ridge Hall Resident Fellow/
Sembawang–Hong Kah CDC Councillor

MY Journey in Politics
Practical Lessons in Leadership

MY Journey in Politics
Practical Lessons in Leadership

Ho Peng Kee

Former Senior Minister of State for Law and Home Affairs, Singapore

World Scientific

NEW JERSEY • LONDON • SINGAPORE • BEIJING • SHANGHAI • HONG KONG • TAIPEI • CHENNAI • TOKYO

Published by

World Scientific Publishing Co. Pte. Ltd.
5 Toh Tuck Link, Singapore 596224
USA office: 27 Warren Street, Suite 401-402, Hackensack, NJ 07601
UK office: 57 Shelton Street, Covent Garden, London WC2H 9HE

Library of Congress Cataloging-in-Publication Data
Names: Ho, Peng Kee, author.
Title: My journey in politics : practical lessons in leadership / Ho Peng Kee,
 Associate Professorial Fellow at National University of Singapore Law School and
 Former Senior Minister of State for Ministry of Law and Ministry of Home Affairs, Singapore.
Description: New Jersey : World Scientific, [2016]
Identifiers: LCCN 2016033481| ISBN 9789813143876 (hardcover) |
 ISBN 9789813143883 (pbk.).
Subjects: LCSH: Ho, Peng Kee. | Politicians--Singapore--Biography. | Government executives--
 Singapore--Biography. | Singapore--Politics and government--1990–
Classification: LCC DS610.73.H6 A3 2016 | DDC 328.5957092 [B] --dc23
LC record available at https://lccn.loc.gov/2016033481

British Library Cataloguing-in-Publication Data
A catalogue record for this book is available from the British Library.

Copyright © 2017 by World Scientific Publishing Co. Pte. Ltd.

All rights reserved. This book, or parts thereof, may not be reproduced in any form or by any means, electronic or mechanical, including photocopying, recording or any information storage and retrieval system now known or to be invented, without written permission from the publisher.

For photocopying of material in this volume, please pay a copying fee through the Copyright Clearance Center, Inc., 222 Rosewood Drive, Danvers, MA 01923, USA. In this case permission to photocopy is not required from the publisher.

Desk Editor: Karimah Samsudin

Typeset by Stallion Press
Email: enquiries@stallionpress.com

DEDICATION

To my parents, Ho Seek Yuen and Chow Lai Heng, who provided for me and shaped my values in the early years

To my wife of 36 years, Choy Ping, who has been a supportive wife and loving mother in all my years in politics

To my daughters, Dawn, Claire and Joanne, who were my constant joy and encouragement to press on

To all the grassroots leaders and residents of Nee Soon East whom I had the privilege to work with to build Nee Soon East to what it is today

To all the staff and volunteers across the many Ministries and agencies, who laboured long and hard with me on many policies and programmes that have made Singapore a better place

And to Jesus Christ, who came into my life in 1976 and has since been my Teacher and Guide

CONTENTS

Dedication		xi
Foreword		xv
Preface		xvii
Prologue		xix
Chapter 1	Initial Years and Life on the Ground	1
Chapter 2	Assuming Political Office	21
Chapter 3	My Work at MinLaw and MHA	39
Chapter 4	Debating in Parliament	75
Chapter 5	Impacting Singaporeans in Other Ways	89
Chapter 6	The 2001 General Elections	119
Chapter 7	Retiring from Political Office	135
Appendix A	My Maiden Speech in Parliament	155
Appendix B	The Nee Soon East Song	165
Appendix C	The Nee Soon East Tagline	167
Appendix D	A Tribute from a Key Grassroots Leader	169

FOREWORD

It is important for those who have helped shape Singapore's development in various fields, whether in government or private sector, to write up their reflections and experiences. This will lead to a storehouse of valuable insights into the way in which we have developed as a nation.

Ho Peng Kee's *My Journey in Politics: Practical Lessons in Leadership* book is a refreshing addition to such books. He was my student in the NUS law school, and later in life, we were colleagues in politics. We were office-holders in two important Ministries — Ministry of Law and Ministry of Home Affairs. As a Senior Minister of State, he worked closely with me on many difficult issues in these two Ministries, some of which he recounts in this book.

He impressed everyone in these Ministries with his dedication and leadership abilities. I could always count on him as a reliable and steady colleague. When we brainstormed issues, he spoke candidly and from his heart. He felt strongly about social issues such as rehabilitation of drug addicts and giving offenders a second chance in life.

He is a very principled man and this comes through in his book. He not only gives an interesting narrative of his life and career but also sets out practical lessons in leadership. These lessons, summarised in a clear manner at the end of each chapter, are useful for those who aspire to take on leadership roles. They are also useful for those who wish to understand the meaning of leadership in our daily lives.

Professor S. Jayakumar

PREFACE

I had completed writing this book by December 2011, seven months after stepping down from politics. Events were fresh in my mind then and I wanted to put my thoughts and feelings on paper. However, it has remained unpublished until now.

I had shown my draft chapters to two persons close to me. After reading some parts, they felt that I should not publish the book as it was. They felt that the book was too self-laudatory with too many "I did this, and I did that!" In writing my memoirs, I never meant to blow my own trumpet. Rather, I felt that I was recording the various things that I did in my 20-year political journey just as they had happened. Still, they had a point. Also, my feelings — whether positive or negative — were somewhat raw. It was better to let the dust settle first. I have rewritten parts of the book since.

Thus, at the outset, I want to say that this book is not about me. It is about the work that many good-hearted men and women, and I together undertook in many arenas that we believed was for the good of Singapore. The quotes set out in the first segment of each chapter gives readers a quick flavor of these diverse arenas as they unfolded over the many years I was in politics. I believe that Singapore has become a better place as a result of the hard work put in by all. This is a key reason why I am sharing this story, which is also *their* story. I was but the catalyst, placed there to provide leadership and guidance. To all these wonderful men and women, both volunteers and staff, I say thank you very much.

I think this book can also serve another purpose. Even though I have never taken any formal courses in leadership or taught leadership courses at the University, I am thankful for the many leadership positions that came my way throughout my life. The first of these came when I was 10 years old; I was appointed class monitor at Primary 4. Since then, in various settings such as school prefectorial board, student council, law faculty student body, football teams, community and civic organisations, church session, national service, student hall of residence, NUS law faculty and so on, I was privileged to have exercised leadership. This book shares — through what I did in the course of my journey in politics — how these leadership experiences had honed and shaped me. It also throws some light on my leadership style and approach. For readers who wish to zoom in on the impact of these experiences, the segment at the end of each chapter titled "Lessons in Leadership" will be useful.

My leadership style and approach is captured in several frameworks. In terms of being a Member of Parliament (MP), I embraced the 4 'A's, i.e., Ability, Accessibility, Affirming nature and Affability. In terms of work, I embraced the 4 'P's, i.e., Professionalism, Personal touch, Pride/Passion, and oPportunity. And in terms of an over-arching philosophy of life, it will be the 4 'C's, i.e., Competence, Confidence, Compassion and Character.

It is my sincere hope that as you read about my journey in politics and community life, these frameworks on being an effective leader and worker, living life well, and touching lives will become real to you too.

Thank you. Enjoy!

PROLOGUE

I became your MP nine months ago. Since then, your grassroots leaders and I have worked hard to create a strong sense of community and belonging in Nee Soon East... I am a firm believer that everyone can do a part, big or small. *I hope that you will do your part...* For a start, I will encourage you to find out more about the good work that your Residents' Committee is doing... If you have suggestions on how to improve good neighbourliness, services or facilities, do let your RC leaders know. Also, do join in the block parties and other RC functions that are organised. These are very good opportunities for me to meet you... I know that Singaporeans are busy people. However, life will be more meaningful if we can help and encourage each other as neighbours... *Together, let's build a stronger Nee Soon East community spirit!*

The above is an extract from my message in the inaugural issue of *Hello Resident*, the constituency newsletter in June 1992. I have put this here where the story of my political journey begins because it has been the warmth, love and support of Nee Soon East residents throughout a memorable 20 years which have undergirded all of my political work.

To them, I say a big 'Thank You'!

I arrived at Professor Jayakumar's (hereafter referred to as Prof Jaya) office at the Old Phoenix Park along Tanglin Road early. His Personal Assistant, Shirley, ushered me into a waiting room. I sat there, not knowing what to expect from our meeting. As it transpired, the meeting changed my life.

Prof Jaya said that PM had asked him to sound me out on this. He then popped the question. "Would you consider standing for election as an MP on the PAP ticket? However, there will be no promise of political office." For a fleeting moment, I baulked. Seeing my reaction, very considerately, he assured me that he did not expect an immediate reply. In fact, he said that the first person I should consult was my wife. Having been in politics, as an older colleague and, indeed, my former Dean, he knew that this would be a life-changer. It was imperative that Choy Ping was supportive. Still, he gently pressed that he hoped I would reply as soon as possible.

The following week, I called Prof Jaya and told him that, having spoken to Choy Ping (although my wife ribs me till today that she cannot quite remember me asking her), I was prepared to throw in my lot. I soon realised why there was some urgency. Our meeting took place sometime in the middle of May. By end August that year, in 1991, the General Elections were called, and I was fielded as one of the 11 new candidates on the PAP ticket!

Life was never the same again.

Chapter 1 | INITIAL YEARS AND LIFE ON THE GROUND

...I sincerely feel that Singaporeans should be more affirming all round, people towards people, people towards Government, Government towards people... What do I mean by affirming? Singaporeans should seek to bring out the best in each other. As we share a common destiny, we also have common accountability and responsibility, one to the other... One expression of mutual affirmation is in our approach towards voicing complaints or criticism... How then may one complain positively? First, balance complaints with compliments. Nothing, and no one is totally bad... Second, there is an art to complaining. Complaints should not demoralise. No doubt, they should have a chastening effect but the overall impact should be one that builds up... Thirdly, if we are complaining against an existing practice or situation, we should consider the alternatives as part of the process of thinking through. We should put ourselves in the position of the other party and empathise with his concerns...

My maiden speech in Parliament, 15 January 1992

Thank you for coming to our Polytechnic to give a talk on *Opportunities of Youth — A Personal Reflection*. The feedback from the students was that they enjoyed listening to your lively account of the significant milestones of your youth. They also liked your 4 'P's formula to success (Professionalism, Passion, oPportunities, Personal touch). It was very gracious of you to accept our lunch invitation, despite your busy schedule. Those of us who had lunch with you enjoyed the easy manner in which you interacted with us, and the lively conversation as well...

Mr Low Wong Fook, Principal of Singapore Polytechnic, 1998

I have had the privilege of sharing with young Singaporeans at several school Speech Days... I encourage them to strive for the 4 'C's — competence, confidence, compassion and character. Schools have an important role to play in helping them attain these 4 'C's... Whilst it is natural for parents to push their children, I hope that the motivation is to help their children realise their full potential — not to beat so and so in class. To me, the starting point must be that we treat each child as a unique individual, with his or her own talents and temperament... Reading is an effective way of bringing the family closer together... Whether one reads on his own or shares with the rest later on, or family members read the same book together, growth takes place. I would encourage all parents, particularly of young children, to make the effort to read to and with their children. For myself, my wife and I have never regretted spending time and effort in reading with our three girls.

My speech at the opening of the 4th Annual Read and Grow Fair,
17 November 1994

Initial Years and Life on the Ground

Even though I had entered the fray only a few months after saying "yes", I attended a "tea session" several years earlier in 1987. I was then Sub-Dean of the Law Faculty and was invited to the late Dr Tay Eng Soon's office (he was then Senior Minister of State for Education) at the Ministry of Education at Kay Siang Road for late afternoon tea. Dr Lee Boon Yang, then Minister for Manpower, was also present. I had earlier shared with Dr Tony Tan, then Minister for Education about the upcoming tea. As Master of Kent Ridge Hall (a student hall of residence in NUS), I hosted Dr Tan at a Hall event. He encouraged me to go for it, but added that I should not be disappointed if nothing came out of it. My sense is that he was concerned that some invitees to these teas may feel really disappointed, or worse, experience rejection or self-doubt if they were not subsequently asked to stand for election on the PAP ticket. I appreciated his thoughtfulness and caring concern. For me, I was not disappointed that nothing came out of that first tea session. After all, the invitation had come out of the blue! Still, that tempered expectation and prepared mindset must have helped some. Not being identified by the PAP through its system of tea sessions was not the be all and end all of one's existence. It was not an indictment or reflection of one's worth as a person, or competence as a professional. Many good candidates could have slipped through the net, even though they may have been considered at one of these teas. Some would say that a few marginal ones have, on the other hand, stood for elections! Indeed, there have been good-hearted Singaporeans who would make good Members of Parliament (MP) who have not been invited to these tea sessions at all, or have declined attending them. It was a necessary, useful, and important process, but not a perfect one.

Thankfully, I entered politics through the 1991 General Elections and not 1988 one. God's timing was perfect! By then, I was a more mature person, having completed one term of three years as the Sub-Dean of the Law Faculty at the National University of Singapore and was in the middle of my term as Vice-Dean. Also, having been Master of Kent Ridge Hall for about three years by then, my experience as Master stood me in very good stead in my early years in politics. As Law Faculty Sub-Dean, I was in charge of student affairs, including overseeing the activities of a very active Student Law Club. At Kent Ridge Hall, I had charge over an active but responsible bunch of 450 students who were positively engaged in student activism. In fact, as I had entered politics a mere three months after agreeing to do so, I had no initiation programme to prepare me for what transpired later. For example, I had no idea what the different 'C's meant, that is "CCC" (Citizens' Consultative Committee), "CC" (Community Centre), "CCMC" (CC Management Committee), "RC" (Residents' Committee), and so on. I attended my first Meet the People session (MPS) only after I became an MP! I had never in my life gone to see an MP at a "Meet the People" session! However, as I shared with the party leaders later, my stint as Resident Fellow and Hall Master — living with and guiding a very active bunch of students at Kent Ridge Hall; and as Sub- and Vice-Dean — interacting with a very active group of students at the Law Faculty — had prepared me well for politics. A key reason was that, with these very active and passionate undergraduates who held strong beliefs in what they were doing, I had to learn to lead and inspire them without stifling their sense of ownership and initiative in the many good projects they were undertaking. It was a fine balance that honed and sharpened my own leadership style that stood me in good stead in my later years in politics. Indeed, interacting and living with active undergraduates, both at the Law Faculty and at Kent Ridge Hall almost throughout my waking hours — both day and night — reflected my personality as someone who likes to mix with people. Entering politics and becoming a Member of Parliament (MP) and office-holder enabled me to do that at the highest level.

At Kent Ridge Hall in particular, we were family. It was communal living at its best, in its most intense form. As Resident Fellow for six years (1981–1987) before becoming the Hall Master, my flat was at the basement of a block of flats that accommodated 110 students. Each time I left or returned home, I had to walk by student rooms in an open courtyard. I often stopped to chat with groups of students sitting by a pond that we had dug and built together. During the examination period, my wife and I would open the door of our flat in the evening so that any student who was feeling anxious, depressed, or just wanted to drop by for a chat could do so. Then, as Master, assisted by a great bunch of Resident Fellows,[1] and working closely with the elected student leaders,[2] we ran one of the most active Halls of Residence on campus. Kent Ridge Hall's Starburst Concert would be long-remembered among NUS students for its vitality and creativity. Kent Ridge Hall alumni include current Judge of Appeal Andrew Phang, former Attorney-General and NMP Walter Woon, former MPs Sin Boon Ann and Sinnakaruppan, playwright Eleanor Wong, singer Dawn Yip, former Miss Singapore Teo Ser Lee, former Permanent Secretary Tan Tee How and many others. Current Chief Justice Sundaresh Menon also benefited from hall life as a resident of neighbouring Sheares Hall.

Significantly, entering politics only in 1991 instead of in 1988 enabled me to secure my Associate Professorship (AP), a key professional milestone, before I crossed over to the front bench as Parliamentary Secretary in 1993. If I had crossed over earlier, it is unlikely that I would have done enough to secure my Associate Professorship! On this score, God's timing was, once again, providential. Prof Jaya informed me that the PM had asked him to sound me out, to find out if I was prepared to take leave from the Law Faculty at NUS, and assume political office full-time sometime in April 1993. About a year before that, sometime in 1992, then NTUC Secretary-General Ong Teng Cheong had asked me to join NTUC full-time. I demurred, explaining to him that even though I was prepared to roll up my sleeves and work full-time to enhance Singaporean workers' interests and welfare, I had planned to take my sabbatical leave over six months in 1992 to write and publish in order to get my Associate Professorship (as at that point in time, I had not published enough). Thankfully, Mr Ong saw where I was coming from and said it was alright. I then proceeded on a local sabbatical in Singapore, published some articles in a few academic journals which, together with my previous publications, teaching record and administrative contributions, tipped the balance towards my promotion as Associate Professor. When I finally took leave from the University in June 1993, the timing was perfect in many ways, not least because I had spent two good years as a backbencher.

In my view, all political office-holders should ideally spend time in the backbench before taking up full-time political office. My time as a backbencher was well-spent. I made speeches in Parliament and at functions, without the constraints of holding political office, and participated in television forums and press discussions. For example, I had a "face off" with Dr Wolfgang Sachsenroeder, then regional director of the Friedrich Naumann Foundation, in *The Straits Times'* Insight column on 23 May 1992, where we debated the topic of "Democracy, East or West?" I also participated in a "Contact Y" programme on television in 1992, where I shared a platform with Dr Vivian Balakrishnan (before he entered politics) on student involvement in politics.[3] I also made many speeches as guest-of-honour at various events, which gave me the opportunity to set out my key concerns as to how Singapore was shaping up as a society.

In my maiden parliamentary speech on 15 January 1992 (*see* Appendix A), I called for a greater sense of appreciation and affirmation among Singaporeans. I made this call when debating the President's Address at the opening of the new session of Parliament. In my final remarks, I adapted what President John F Kennedy, in his inauguration speech in 1963, had said. I asked Singaporeans to "not just ask what the Government can do for you". Adding that while that was a legitimate question and Singaporeans were right in asking it, I urged Singaporeans to also ask "what, as fellow Singaporeans we can do for one another." Interestingly, the sentiments underlying these words were echoed in one of the last speeches I made as office-holder and MP on 29 March 2011. I had only realised this several months later when looking through my materials for this book. The occasion was the annual Prisons-SCORE[4] work plan seminar, where key leaders and volunteers from a range of agencies and voluntary welfare organisations were present. As I did in 1992, I ended my speech with a clarion call to Singaporeans to participate actively in building an engaged and energised society.[5] On my early call for Singaporeans to be more affirming, *The Straits Times*, in an article on 19 August 2006, when recalling the highlights of its by then defunct "Off-the-Record" column, highlighted my love for the word:

> When he made his debut as a politician in 1991, he called on Singaporeans to be "more affirming to one another". Asked to describe himself later, he said he was "warm, caring and affirming". And when suggesting a theme for the courtesy campaign, he offered, yes, you guessed it, "affirming and encouraging one another".

Early impressions linger on and form a lasting image of a politician, for better or for worse!

Other speeches I made in Parliament as a backbencher and at functions helped to define my political persona as I passionately spoke up for causes I believed in. At functions, I spoke mainly from the heart in tandem with the function's setting. It was heart-warming and humbling that quite a few of my hosts told me that my extempore remarks were the ones that struck them more than what I said from the prepared text. Dr R Theyvendran, Secretary-General of the Management Development Institute of Singapore (MDIS) wrote to me in October 2000, saying: "your impromptu speech truly reflected an excellent mind — and touching words, which came from the heart..."[6] After I had graced the Presentation of the Schools' West Coast Sports Colours Awards in 1994, Chairperson Madam Lau Kan How wrote: "The students were thrilled to hear about your personal experiences and were inspired by your dedication to sports." Richard Dawson, then Principal of Woodlands Secondary School, wrote in August 1994: "The staff and students were very much taken by your warmth and personable approach. They found your address, especially the three 'C's to be stimulating and appropriate."[7] A final example which I felt particularly honoured to receive came from Eugene Wijeysingha, former Principal of Raffles Institution. In November 1994, he wrote: "I read with great interest the speeches you make in your official capacity, at various functions, because they stem from a very warm human heart."[8] My desire to connect and leave a positive impression when speaking extended to the times I was Government representative at a foreign country's National Day reception in Singapore. I had asked Prof Jaya in 2003 whether it was alright for me to say a few words before I offered the formal toast.[9] In his usual affirming way, Prof Jaya replied that there was no harm saying a few words in response, and with his wry humour added: "But don't forget to propose the toast"! With this, the formal part of the celebration became less stiff and hopefully, more meaningful for the guests, as when I commended the South Africans for their unity, passion, and incredible hospitality when staging the FIFA World Cup in 2010.[10]

Parliament is an excellent platform for a newly-elected backbench Member of Parliament (MP) to raise his key concerns. Some issues that I spoke up on were ensuring that the Gifted Education Programme did not produce students who were too individualistic, encouraging greater involvement on the part of our students in co-currricular activities (CCA) as these were important for their all-round development, getting more Singaporeans to sign up as volunteers in our fight against crime and drugs, and preserving our heritage and leveraging on it to bridge the intergenerational gap. At the 1993 Committee of Supply debate, I spoke passionately for the establishment of a Sports Ministry, arguing that Singapore needed a supremo in sports, much as it had champions in the arts, like then Minister George Yeo and Professor Tommy Koh. I repeated this call a few months later at a dialogue session conducted by the Feedback Unit. Using a wheel analogy, I outlined nine spokes of the wheel that together, I felt, would make sports tick in Singapore.[11] My speech in Parliament made it as the "Speech of the day" in the following day's *The Straits Times*.¹² I remember vividly what a former colleague who ran the sports department at the National University of Singapore for many years said to me a few days after I made my speech. He applauded my efforts but said I should not waste my time. At that time, many in the sporting fraternity held up little hope that Government would invest more resources into sports. However, much to our delight, in the year 2000, the Government renamed the Ministry of Community Development as the Ministry of Community Development, Youth and Sports. I hope that my speech and other efforts on the playing field as well as my interactions with the then Singapore Sports Council had, in some way, helped to bring this about.

Tommy Koh is an exceptional Singaporean who has made his mark in many areas of public life, in and outside Singapore. For me, an early impression was back in 1980, when, as a young NUS law lecturer pursuing a Masters in Law at Harvard Law School, I had visited the United Nations HQ in New York. By impulse, I thought I should call on Tommy, who was then our permanent representative to the UN. With little hesitation, he agreed to see me. I found his approachability and informality refreshing and inspiring.

As a backbencher, an MP can lobby hard on worthy causes or appeal repeatedly on deserving cases to the relevant office-holders. These actions help to establish his standing with his constituents and credibility as their representative in Parliament. Framing an appeal in the strongest terms possible also sensitises him to the difficulties faced by these residents. This, in turn, prepares him for life as an office-holder when he sits at the opposite end considering these appeals. In this sense, it is a pity that many of today's office-holders have had no prior experience as a backbencher.

It was interesting that when my candidacy was announced, the media highlighted the fact that I was a committed Christian and also a church elder. I did not go out of my way to make this fact known, and neither did I attempt to suppress it. I suppose in the context of "hard-headed" PAP politics (back in 1991), the media found it interesting that the PAP had decided to field a person like me — someone who was not hard-nosed; had no prior links with the Party or grassroots bodies; a law academic who had decided to teach at the University instead of practise at the Bar; someone who made it clear that it was his conviction that Singapore needed to become a more compassionate, caring society, and a committed, practising church elder to boot! However, I am thankful that my faith was publicised at the outset. This way, my residents and grassroots leaders knew my stand from the beginning, that in performing my duties as MP to all my residents from the different faiths and races, I would work hard to the best of my ability but would not do anything which I felt would compromise my faith. Hence, they understood when I did not hold joss sticks or burn incense in the Chinese temples (although I had no qualms visiting them for dialogue sessions or celebration dinners).

All MPs in Singapore have to run their constituencies well. Even if he were a strong Minister with a good track record in the Ministry he was in charge of, it was his record as MP and the residents' familiarity with him on the ground that ultimately counts in a General Election, especially a closely-contested one. This was an important lesson that the PAP learnt in the 2011 General Elections (GE), but got it right in the intervening years before the recent 2015 GE, when it won with a big vote swing of almost 10% (from 60.1% in 2011 to 69.9% in 2015). A key catchphrase of all MPs now, whether Government or Opposition, is to "serve the residents"! On this, I must confess that I had studiously avoided saying to my residents that I was there to serve them. For sure, there was an element of service in what an MP does on the ground. However, in my time, I felt that saying it in those stark terms was too one-sided. It sent the wrong message that all that my residents needed to do was to "wait and be served", or worse, just complain if the service was not up to their expectations! Instead, my constant refrain was: "Let's work together to build a better, stronger Nee Soon East"; that is, while I would certainly do my part, they should do theirs too — for example, to keep the neighbourhood clean; to foster better neighbourliness; to join in the grassroots activities; to help deter crime, and so on. Still, I can understand why all MPs now, whether Opposition or Government, feel they have to say that they are there to serve their residents. Circumstances have changed. Voters' expectations have been created and must be met.

My key point is that every MP, especially a first-term MP, must diligently and sincerely work the ground. There are no shortcuts. Drawing on my experience as hall resident fellow and master, law faculty Sub-Dean and Vice-Dean as well as church elder, I set out to connect with residents from Day One, concentrating first on the residents' committees in each of the zones. I was taking a leaf from my experience in running Kent Ridge Hall, where each of the five blocks was looked after by a Resident Fellow who lived with the students. Being a University professor, contrary to popular thinking at that time, actually helped my cause. This was because I was not a typical law professor. Instead of dying to see my name on a book or article, I was an activist who enjoyed meeting and hamming it up with students (as a law don and hall master), and with residents (as MP) from all backgrounds. I smiled easily, shook hands freely and sincerely (no loose handshakes for me), patted backs or squeezed shoulders and elbows occasionally (although my family thinks that I overdo this), and enjoyed brisk-walking, running, cycling and playing games with grassroots leaders and residents. Here, again, I think the media found me quite unusual, resulting in unusually good coverage of my ground activities in my ward, Nee Soon East, which was then part of Sembawang Group Representative Constituency (GRC) in the early days. Some were accompanied by good photo opportunities that caught readers' eyes. Thus, I was pictured in the media in various poses and wearing a range of apparel, from in-line blading gear to swimming trunks to football shorts, jersey and boots, to running gear. I was pictured cycling with my grassroots leaders, wearing a turban, and also saying a few words in Hindi or Tamil. The press also carried old school photographs of me hurdling, debating, and acting. All these pictures helped to "humanise" me as a politician, casting me as "one of the boys", and by implication, someone who understood the anxieties and concerns of residents on the ground.

Throughout my tenure as MP from 1991 to 2011, it was my privilege to have looked after Nee Soon East (NSE), first as a ward in Sembawang GRC and then, from 2001, as a Single-Member Constituency (SMC). In particular, the last 10 years when NSE was an SMC were especially memorable ones. I daresay that an enduring highlight of my political career was to have created a vibrant community spirit among NSE residents, strong bonds among grassroots leaders, and a sense of shared destiny and common purpose among all who worked in the constituency, helping to make it a caring and cosy place for all. We adopted an informal, interactive approach to addressing many of the local issues, such as the lack of carpark lots, presence of foreign workers living in nearby dormitories, road safety issues, building of new amenities, creating more football fields and open spaces, and lift upgrading of the few low-rise flats in Nee Soon East which ordinarily would not have been upgraded. Working closely with the relevant agencies, nobody stood on ceremony, and everyone worked sincerely and passionately towards resolving these local issues. Hence, when I attended our many grassroots functions such as block parties organised by the Residents' Committee, or disco nights organised by the Malay Activities Executive Committee, or our very popular Children's Day celebrations at our amphitheatre, my standing instructions to the organisers was not to ask anyone to stand up on my arrival but to just announce my arrival, not as Minister, but as grassroots adviser or MP, and let things take its course. Some residents stood, while others did not, which was alright with me. Also, on arriving at the event, instead of heading for a seat at the front row, I would walk around informally, shaking hands and chatting with everyone present. I much preferred a casual, informal atmosphere. In fact, I told my grassroots leaders that if everyone present was warm and friendly, then we were not reaching out enough to our detractors!

As we were family in Kent Ridge hall, so also were we family in Nee Soon East (NSE). The NSE family included the Principals of the seven schools in the constituency (probably the highest number of schools in a single ward or constituency at that time), staff of relevant agencies like the Housing and Development Board, Town Council, Land Transport Authority, Constituency Secretariat, National Environment Agency, National Library Board, and Neighbourhood Police Post/Centre, as well as staff and volunteers of Voluntary Welfare Organisations (VWOs) that had centres or offered services in Nee Soon East, such as the Student Care Services, Evangel Family Church, Yishun Chinese Combined Temple, Darul Makmur Mosque, Chung Hwa Free Clinic and Salem Church. Together with my key volunteer leaders, chief of whom were Chris Lim Ah Lek and Ng Yam Boon (CCC chairmen), K Gopal (Branch Secretary), William Choo (a rare[13] "outside" friend I had brought into Nee Soon East who chaired the Community Centre Management Committee), and Ahmad Karim (who was active in my Meet the People Session and the constituency's sports activities), we built up Nee Soon East. Other grassroots leaders who also played key roles were Lawrence Koh, Jaffar Hashim, Barbara Lee, Nancy Goh, Kumari Devi, Tan Meng, Eric Woon, Betty Lai, Michael Tan, Andrew Ng, Ramli Kasiman, Rose Koh, Alfred Koh, Hassan Bek, Ang Kieow Mok, and Choo Kim Boon. My Constituency Senior Manager, Leow Meng Hong, helped me to pull everything together. Early on in June 1992, we launched our very own newsletter aptly titled *Hello Resident*, and composed our very own constituency song, sung in the four official languages (*see* Appendix B). I had asked a former ACS schoolmate, Tony Wei, who was then Director of the SAF Music and Drama Company, to compose the song. We also had our own tagline, "We Love Nee Soon East", which I would rally the residents with at our many community functions, again in our four official languages (*see* Appendix C).

At these functions, I usually addressed the many children gathered there directly, for example, encouraging them to be good children, to listen to their parents, and to love their siblings. I think I struck a chord with these children by "coming down to their level", sometimes physically, by squatting down when talking to them or sitting with them when watching magic shows and other performances. Indeed, it was a real joy for me to see many of our children in Nee Soon East growing up over the years to become young men and women who had happy memories growing up in Nee Soon East. In my many farewell events before I stepped down from office in May 2011, I met many of them who unabashedly asked me if I still remembered them — from the time we had taken a photograph together at their PAP Community Foundation kindergarten graduation ceremonies to the many Children's Days' functions we held at our Nee Soon East Courtyard to the regular block parties organised years earlier. These heartening moments always caused a lump to swell in my throat and tears to brim in my eyes! Even after my retirement from politics, a young person would occasionally come up to me to introduce himself or herself as someone I had shaken hands with in Nee Soon East as a child.

Another way I sought to bond with my residents was by engaging in sports with them, especially through football. The language of sports is universal, spanning ages, races and backgrounds, and a very effective way of getting to know the residents. Every time I donned my sports gear and mixed it up with them, I think I created a lasting impression that far surpassed any speech I made could have done. To be identified with them, where they were, in a natural setting was something they appreciated. To foster racial harmony, I urged everyone to pick up a few phrases in each other's languages, and led the way by learning some phrases myself, which I would use during my informal speeches at functions. For example, we would learn to say "hello" or "good morning", or count the numbers one to 10, in Malay, Tamil, and Mandarin.

I do not think my limited grasp of Hokkien in any way hampered my outreach to my residents, including the older Chinese ones. Most understood Mandarin, even if some could not speak it well. Over the years, with tuition and 95.8 FM on the radio as my constant travelling companion when I drove (thanks to the crew there, especially "the Old Master, Qiu Shengyang" 邱胜扬), residents of Nee Soon East could see that I was trying hard to improve my spoken Mandarin. They appreciated this which, in turn, enhanced our connection on the ground. Many of them commented that I had made good progress. (Actually, I did well for Chinese as my second language at the 'O' levels in 1970, scoring a B3 grade, despite being in Anglo Chinese School, where the badge of honour among the students was to do badly in Chinese!) The key is sincerity in interaction with residents. Residents can be touched by sincere warm wishes conveyed in "broken" Malay, a few phrases in Tamil, or basic Mandarin. Indeed, early on, a key leader in the merchants' committee at that time taught me to sing a rousing Mandarin chorus that extolled "strength in unity" (团结就是力量 or "tuan jie jiu shi li liang"). From then on, I would say that I had many teachers among my grassroots leaders who taught me Mandarin and some Hokkien. In this way, I recognised their contributions and affirmed them, attributing the positive results of my interactions with residents, especially the older ones who did not speak English, to their efforts.

In short, we dared to do things differently in Nee Soon East. This mindset led us to explore new approaches; for example, in 1992, I sent a note to new residents inviting them to have tea with me, held a monthly free legal counselling clinic, and also tapped my personal contacts to organise talks for residents[14] and to form a Transport Study Team that improved traffic flow to and in Nee Soon East.[15] Later, we organised a large-scale lion dance competition in the heartlands,[16] worked with the Society for the Prevention of Cruelty to Animals (SPCA) to organise a pets' carnival at our Community Club, and built (at that time) the largest HDB heartlands games hard court. Recognising that Belgians cycled a lot, when we hosted the visit of His Excellency Yves Leterme, Minister-President of Flanders of the Kingdom of Belgium to the constituency in November 2005, we arranged for him, together with his entourage, myself and a few key grassroots leaders, to cycle around the constituency, in conjunction with the annual Clean and Green Week. On our tour of Nee Soon East, we visited the many sites where trees had been planted in earlier Clean and Green Week activities. Our visitors found our time together very interesting![17] Moreover, in everything we did, we had the interest and welfare of our residents at heart. We were family where everyone mattered. That we largely succeeded in Nee Soon East to build rapport with residents and a collective sense of belonging and community spirit is borne out by the fact that in the last General Election that I fought in 2006, Nee Soon East achieved the fourth best overall results for any PAP ward, and the best result by any PAP MP against the main Opposition party, the Workers' Party. Even in the 2001 General Elections, when Nee Soon East became the most hotly-contested constituency at the hustings, I scored a creditable victory over a credible opponent, Dr Poh Lee Guan, then Assistant Secretary-General of the Worker's Party, garnering 73.68% of the votes cast.

Indeed, I spent so much time on the ground in Nee Soon East that it became my second home!

To give readers a sense of this, set out below in the January 2006 issue of *Hello Resident* is my schedule over two weeks in 2005 at Nee Soon East:

Sunday (25 September)	Neighbourhood 4 market visit, followed by block party at Zone 1
Monday (26 September)	Meet the People session
Thursday (27 September)	House to house visit
Saturday (28 September)	Children's Day Celebration at the Sports Park
Monday (3 October)	Meet the People session
Tuesday (4 October)	Photo-taking with NSE PAP Community Foundation (PCF) Kindergarten 2 children
Friday (7 October)	PCF Sparkletots (childcare centre) "Phonics and Rhymes" concert
Sunday (9 October)	Block Party at Zone 5

Lessons in Leadership

1. As a newly-installed leader, it is important to come across as an earnest learner and sincere listener. Never disparage your predecessor's work. Recognise the good work that has been done. However, be aware of the weaknesses and outstanding problems without accentuating them. Be prepared to roll up your sleeves to tackle these with fresh vigour and new insights. You must be able to win the trust and confidence of the people you "inherit", especially that of the "old-timers". Introduce your "own people" from outside the organisation strategically and thoughtfully. Ideally, space them out. Be mindful of the diverse groups of people you may be dealing with. This is where good social quotient comes into play.
2. A new leader must also be able to establish his own credibility quickly. Here, there is no substitute for hard work and sincerity. Be mindful of the perceptions that others who do not yet know you well may have of you, based on your background; for example, in my case, as an "ivory tower" academic detached from ground reality. If there is such a negative perception, show that you are different. Still, recognise your core strengths and shortcomings, and always be yourself; do not pretend to be what you are not. As a leader, you should be comfortable with the type of leadership you project. This can only be the case if you are honest with yourself and are true to your character.
3. Embrace creativity as you lead. Try new ways of doing things. Bring value to the organisation you join or lead. Weave in your own experience, contacts, insights, and "grow the pie". As you do so, ensure that you do not overwhelm those you lead with these new ideas. Win their acceptance and trust, as you enliven and strengthen the organisation. Get their buy-in by involving them.
4. It will be useful for a leader to know a bit about psychology. It is an important soft skill and is a key component in nurturing emotional quotient (EQ). This will enable you to understand

people better. For me, studying literature as a subject in school up to 'A' levels has been helpful. It has enabled me to understand human emotions a little better. What makes a person tick? What would move a person to supporting someone as a leader? What may be some of the things — words, actions and so on — that may put off a potential supporter? How can you motivate a volunteer?

Endnotes

1. These included Dr Ting Seng Kiong, John Ang, Dr Ong Bee Lian, Dr Loo Yeow Hwa, Tan Wee Liang, Dr Rosalind Phang, Dr Yap Chee Meng, Dr Andrew Wee, and Dr Gary Yeo. Domestic Manager, Thomas Ling was an icon, holding that position from 1979 to 2003, and working with several Masters and countless batches of student leaders, many of whom got to know him very well.
2. The student leaders in the Junior Common Room Committee (JCRC) were elected by the students living in the hall. Two outstanding JCRC Presidents I had worked with were Koh Kok Hong and Koh Kew Sek.
3. Vivian Balakrishnan entered politics in 2001. He is now Minister for Foreign Affairs. The programme's producer, later in her "Thank You" note, wrote that "the feedback we got was that it was an engaging discussion and many interesting points were raised by both yourself and Vivian…"
4. "SCORE" refers to the Singapore Corporation of Rehabilitative Enterprises.
5. See *TODAY*, 30 March 2011. As is usually the case with my speeches, my rallying call made at the end of my speech comprised extempore, "off the cuff" remarks from my heart. There was no text that I can quote. However, TODAY's report said that I had emphasised the importance of community support. I also said that the greatest satisfaction lay in whether one had been an agent of change, quoting me as saying that "to me, that is a high calling". My closing remarks were that "throughcare — a seamless process from rehabilitation to reintegration — was the next challenge".
6. I was Guest-of-Honour at MDIS' Scholarship and Bursary Award Presentation.
7. The occasion was the School's Speech and Prize-giving Day on 20 August 1992. The three 'C's I spoke about were "Competence, Compassion and Character", which I exhorted the students to embrace and exhibit in their own lives. I had made this call at many of the schools I spoke at during those early years as MP. In later speeches, I added a fourth 'C' — Confidence.
8. I had known Eugene Wijeysingha when we served together on the National Police Cadet Corps Council. He was then Headmaster of

Raffles Institution and was himself renowned to be an eloquent and persuasive speaker.
9. Hitherto, as far as I know, the Government representative would not say much, if anything at all, proceeding to return the official toast after the host Ambassador had made his.
10. This was at the South Africa Celebration of Freedom Day on 27 April 2011.
11. See *The Straits Times* report, 1 July 1993. The nine spokes comprised committed athletes, NSAs manned by passionate volunteers engaging coaches who make things happen, bigger role for the Singapore Sports Council, Government providing the facilities, emphasizing sports that Singapore can excel in, society that accepts the nation-building role of sports, supportive employers and sponsors, affirming media and lastly parents, teachers and schools to help identify and nurture raw talents. That was the ecosystem I had argued for.
12. 19 March 1993.
13. The only other notable "outside" friend I had brought into Nee Soon East was Tan Tee Jim. Tee Jim was my NJC and law faculty classmate at the Singapore University. Despite his busy and successful legal career, he agreed to be the Constituency Sport Club's Patron.
14. Speakers included the late Anthony Yeo (then director of Care and Counselling Centre) who talked about "Handling Conflicts", Lim Yen Lan (Past President of the Singapore Association for Women's Lawyers) who talked about "The Women's Charter" and Professor Wee Chow Hou (then NUS Professor) who talked about "Sun Tzu's Art of War".
15. I got a NUS colleague specialising in transportation engineering, Dr Chin Hoong Chor, to chair this Committee. A key improvement made by this study team was reconfiguration to a key junction at Lentor Avenue 2/Yishun Ring Road. It is good to see that this key junction has since been further improved. Other improvements included creating more carpark space, improvements to bus routes and bus schedules, and provision of turning lanes for cars at road junctions. This team continued to exist throughout my 20 years in Nee Soon East, even though the personnel changed from time to time. It greatly facilitated discussion with LTA, bus service provides, PWD and other relevant agencies, which led to continuing

improvements to our transport infrastructure and services in the constituency.
16. This was jointly organised with the Singapore National Wushu Federation in 2007. Hitherto, a competition of this magnitude was only organised at Takashimaya Square along Orchard Road, not in the HDB heartlands.
17. The event was reported in the January 2006 issue (pp. 6–7) of the constituency newsletter, *Hello Resident*, available online at http://www.neesooneast.com.

Chapter 2 — ASSUMING POLITICAL OFFICE

Achieving something in life is not unlike scoring a goal at the end of a surging run in football. Some of you, like me, have experienced that feeling. Everything must be just right. You must see the opportunity coming, run to open space, call for the ball, your first touch must be right as the ball is played to you, beat the defender, look up briefly to see where the goalkeeper is and either drive, lob or tap the ball into the net. Your reward is to see the net bulge as the ball hits the net... But behind every spectacular goal lies a lot of hard work, patience and sometimes, tedious practice and training.

> Speaking to ITE students at the 3rd ITE Student Seminar
> on 21 September 2001

They normally walk the corridors of power. Yesterday, they showed what it took to pack a power walk on public roads. Prior planning was required: coordinated outfits, complete with their team name, Jaya Walkers, printed on their T-shirts... Prof Jaya showed where his power centre really lies — in his *gelek* (shake for Malay). He sported the determined style of a competitive walker, elbows swaying briskly, legs moving apace. R(Adm)Teo stood out for being Mr Long Legs. A head and shoulders above the crowd, he wore the relaxed expression of one on a Sunday stroll in the park. But his long strides ate up the 10-kilometre like a moving missile... Prof Ho was struggling behind. The ministers looked back several times to keep an eye out for Prof Ho... Where was Mr Wong? Mr Wong had raced away upon flag-off at 7.30 a.m. The rest of the team didn't see him until 9.00 a.m. at the finish line... When the leaders met at the finish line, Prof Jayakumar gripped Mr Wong's arm playfully and said with a smile: "He wants to prove he is Leader of the House."

> *The New Paper* coverage on 22 May 1995 on the TNP Big Walk

We were stunned on receiving the letter of approval. Our joy is beyond description. You have given us hope; a sense of security and assurance of success in life. We have peace of mind to make our utmost contribution to the country of Singapore which we love dearly.

> From a family who was granted long-term stay in Singapore

Assuming Political Office

In June 1993, I was appointed Parliamentary Secretary at the Ministry of Home Affairs (MHA) and the Ministry of Law (MinLaw). I was promoted to Senior Parliamentary Secretary in January 1996, to Minister of State a year later in January 1997, and to Senior Minister of State in June 2001, serving in the two Ministries for 18 years in all. I stepped down from that office in May 2011. When I assumed political office in 1993, I took leave from NUS and vacated the Master's Residence at Kent Ridge Hall, moving first into my mother's flat for a while before moving into my own house which had been rented out before. That meant a loss of income. Taking that into account, I took a pay-cut when I assumed full-time political office. However, this never figured in my mind, as I relished and looked forward to the opportunity to serve on a wider and higher platform.

Some of my friends had expressed disappointment that I was not promoted as full Minister in the Cabinet. This was especially so after the 2001 General Elections, when then Prime Minister Goh Chok Tong had, in responding to the media, said that in appointing a Minister of Law, I would be one of those he would consider. I was there when he said that. Unlike these friends however, I never took that to mean that he was thinking of appointing me to the position. Rather, from a practical viewpoint, he had stated the obvious, that is, if he were to appoint a Law Minister, he would consider those who were legally trained, including Mr Lee Kuan Yew, Prof Jaya (then the incumbent) and me.[1] At best, the most favourable interpretation would be that, at least, I crossed the threshold to be considered; that is, I had the potential to be the Law Minister. I certainly did not see his words as any indication of a promotion, let alone a promise! Still, what was reassuring was that Mr Goh was reported to have said that I was "an important part of Singapore's third-generation leaders."[2]

I was therefore not disappointed at all when this did not materialise. Moreover, Mr Goh had made the remark in the cut and thrust of election hustings, and it should be looked at in that context. The way I look at it is that he was trying to speak up for me, putting me in the best light possible, but without misleading anyone or promising anything. Still, the way the media reported his remark caused many to think otherwise. Indeed, Prof Jaya, then my boss at the Ministry of Law, emailed me that night saying that what he had heard on the news earlier was "excellent", that PM "considers you as a future Minister for Law to succeed me". Still, I was under no illusion at all that I would be promoted to the Cabinet, especially as Minister for Law or Minister for Home Affairs.

In fact, that I could rise as high as I did despite my background is a credit to the system. As I had explained in Chapter 1, my nomination as MP probably came as a surprise to some people who held a hard-nosed view of PAP politics. I was not a government scholar, nor was I from the civil service or armed forces. Quite the opposite, I was a university don who was open about his faith and wore his feelings on his sleeves! There was no promise of political office when I first entered politics in 1991. However, after I entered the system as an MP, my potential was probably recognised and I was appointed to office at a junior level as Parliamentary Secretary. In fact, this happened because the late Dr Ong Chit Chung (then Senior Parliamentary Secretary of Home Affairs and Labour) had decided to return to the private sector while remaining as MP, thus creating a vacancy. In a sense, my elevation to the front bench was fortuitous!

Working very closely with two very senior Ministers, I am thankful that my contribution and abilities were recognised. I was duly rewarded with several promotions to a rank just below that of a Cabinet Minister. Quite accurately, the system was true to itself and recognised that I would not fit in as well as a Cabinet Minister in charge of Law and Home Affairs. This is a correct assessment, as I do not have an essential ingredient for someone occupying that office — a hard edge. For any team, including the Cabinet, to function effectively, the right man or woman must be found for the right job. The Minister for Law or Minister for Home Affairs must necessarily be the person who will strike, and strike hard, for

Singapore and the government, especially in relation to overseas critics, when the need arises. As such, he must have a tough edge. If any member of the team should be the person to create fear or apprehension in its opponents, if the need ever arises, either the Minister for Law or the Minister for Home Affairs is that man. I did not fit the bill as I lacked the "killer instinct". My natural instinct was to "affirm and build a person up" rather than to "tear him down". Still, as my many encounters in Parliament showed, especially in taking the Motions and Parliamentary Questions filed by Mr Jeyaretnam when he returned to the House as Non-Constituency MP (NCMP) between 1997 and 2001, I demonstrated that I could be firm and stand my ground, if necessary — at least, in terms of my substantive arguments, responses and rebuttals.

In fact, in 1997, when I was informed that I had been promoted to Minister of State for Law and Minister of State for Home Affairs, I had asked then PM Goh Chok Tong in his office if I had a chance to make it to the Cabinet as full Minister. His reply was frank and candid. He said that, at that point in time, he did not see me as a Cabinet Minister, but I recall him adding that anything could happen. My response was that while I did not see myself as a Minister for Law or Minister for Home Affairs, I felt that I could do the job and would add value to Cabinet as Minister for Community Development, Youth and Sports. There was no Ministry of Social and Family Development (MSF) then, another portfolio I could have added value to. Unlike the Cabinet Ministers who were my peers such as Messrs Teo Chee Hean, George Yeo, Lim Hng Kiang and Lim Swee Say, I was not a government scholar.[3] I went through life as many other Singaporeans. Having studied at the Anglo Chinese School and the National Junior College (I was a very active student at both ACS and NJC), I made many life-long friends. I completed two and half years of national service together with others in non-scholar platoons, receiving my commission as a second lieutenant in February 1974. Before assuming full-time political office in 1993, I had completed my cycle of eight high-key reservist in-camp training, holding the rank of an infantry captain. I studied at the then Singapore University, a local University where, again, as an active student in sports, debates, and student leadership, I made many friends across the faculties. As a Law don and NUS Hall Resident Fellow/Master for 14 and 11 years respectively, I interacted with thousands of bright university students across the disciplines, quite a few of whom I would meet up again later in politics. These contacts helped me to keep a strong pulse on the ground. With this background, I would have complemented the PSC scholar, government service or armed forces backgrounds (all needed in our political system) of the other Cabinet Ministers who were my peers. Moreover, unlike the others who had studied engineering or computer science, I had switched from the Science stream to the Arts stream when I was enrolled in NJC.[4] I enjoyed subjects such as history (which gave me a better understanding of the present world) and literature (a microcosm of life where emotions and relationships are explored in depth). Indeed, as office-holder, whenever the opportunity arose, I would extol the study of literature, which I felt should be encouraged in our schools so as to produce all-rounded students who could better appreciate the full range of human emotions and how these shaped a person's motivations and actions.

In retrospect, I am thankful that I was not made a Cabinet Minister. Life would have been very different had that been the case. For 18 years as an office-holder in the two Ministries, I worked with two very senior Ministers who both later became Deputy Prime Ministers. For a long time, there was no second Minister working alongside us,[5] which effectively made me the *de facto* second Minister. At MHA, at different points in time, Senior Parliamentary Secretary Maidin Packer and Political Secretary Harun Ghani, played key roles in reaching out to the Malay ground in our fight against drugs and crime. Shortly before I retired, Masagos Zulkifli was promoted to Minister of State at MHA. He had joined MHA as Senior Parliamentary Secretary in 2006 upon election as MP. I remain grateful to these colleagues for shouldering their share of the the load at MHA.

Both Prof Jaya and Mr Wong Kan Seng had heavy additional responsibilities as they wore other hats as well. Prof Jaya was, for many years, when I was with him at the Ministry of Law, also the Minister for Foreign Affairs. He therefore travelled often. Once a year when the United Nations General Assembly was in session in New York (normally in September or October), he would usually be away for about two to three weeks. Mr Wong was in charge of the People's Association, oversaw all of the PAP's party affairs as First Assistant Secretary-General, and also helmed a high-level Steering Committee as co-chairman with the PRC's Vice-Premier, overseeing economic relations between Singapore and China. I was an active Number Two who worked very closely with them. As such, I am thankful that I was in a position to influence the shaping of many key policies, and officiated at many Ministry functions and events. In retrospect, I had the best perch, being at the heart of politics as the right-hand man to two very senior Ministers, right in the thick of the action but not fully absorbed into it.

I enjoyed working alongside Prof Jaya and Mr Wong. At both the Ministry of Law and Ministry of Home Affairs, I would like to think that I complemented them in what they did. At MinLaw, I was a younger, more energetic person. My relaxed disposition enabled me to mix easily on the ground with everyone alike. MinLaw's statutory bodies and departments, especially the Intellectual Property Office of Singapore (IPOS), Singapore Land Authority and Community Mediation Unit, found me a useful Guest-of-Honour (GOH) who could further their outreach and causes without fuss at events on the ground. Hence, I officiated at many of their functions, often making extempore remarks on top of my prepared speech so as to energise the audience and better connect them with these causes. I was also intimately involved in MinLaw's various staff events such as the annual Work Improvement Teams (WITs) competition (I was the GOH for many years and donated a challenge trophy that bore my name), and the annual ACTIVE Day (a day dedicated to promoting healthy lifestyle and regular exercise), where I donned a T-shirt and a pair of shorts, and joined other MinLaw staff in games and the occasional treasure hunt!

I must say that, at least once, I was overly-enthusiastic at these events. This is how I have become slightly deaf in my right ear! This happened when I struck a gong too hard at an event organised by the Singapore Mediation Centre. This was in July 2007 at the Opening Ceremony of an International Negotiation Competition for Law Students held at the Supreme Court. As Guest-of-Honour on that occasion, I was not required to make a speech. All I had to do was to go on stage to strike a gong to signify the start of the event. When invited to do so, I eagerly bounded up the stage. Enthusiastically, I made some extempore remarks to reach out to and connect with the students (this was to make up for not having to make a speech). Then, just as enthusiastically, I took the striking stick and struck the gong with some force with my right hand. As I did so, I bent over (this shows how hard I was striking it), turning my head towards the left. The resounding gong reverberated strongly into my right eardrum and damaged it. Shortly after that, at the reception, I knew that I was in trouble as I could hardly hear what my host was saying! Till today, this hearing defect has stayed with me. Talk about occupational hazards!

Apart from MinLaw-initiated events, for many years, I was also active in the annual Law Awareness Week organised by the Law Society to promote the pro bono spirit among lawyers and to reach out to the public. In addition, I became the "Government face" in key overseas meetings such as the once-in-three-years Commonwealth Law Ministers' Meeting (CLMM) that took me to far-flung places such as Trinidad and Tobago, St Vincent and the Grenadines, Ghana and Edinburgh, the biennial ASEAN Law Ministers' meeting (ALMM) and the Intellectual Property Office of Singapore's (IPOS) annual conferences with its Chinese counterpart in Beijing and Shanghai.

Prof Jaya knew me well from my university days, where he was first my teacher and then my boss, as Dean of the Law Faculty. I still remember him walking into my office on the first day of work at both the NUS in 1979 (when I had returned to teach at the Law Faculty on his invitation after spending three memorable weeks at Allen & Gledhill as their only pupil from the Singapore University that year, all ready to join the firm on completion of pupillage;

Mr Booker, their top partner at that time was shocked at my decision to leave the firm to return to teach at the Law Faculty, storming into the firm's library where I was doing some research to tell me so), and at MHA in 1993, when we were at the old Phoenix Park. At NUS, Prof Jaya had sauntered into my office to welcome me back to the Faculty and to ask how I was settling in; very reassuring when it comes from your boss on the first day of work! Likewise, he walked into my office at MHA in June 1993 (he was then Minister for Home Affairs and Minister for Law), welcomed me to the Ministry and set his old golf clubs, all in place in a nice golf bag, before me. With a wry smile, he said that I must learn to play golf. Talk about pressure! Of course, I appreciated the warm gesture and useful suggestion; such was the warmth of the man (unfortunately, this is the side of him that many among the public did not readily see and appreciate).

At MinLaw's former office at Raffles City, he even let me occupy Mr EW Barker's old office, which was a much bigger office than the one he was using (he had continued using that smaller office from the time he had moved in as Second Minister when Mr Barker was Minister). I think he was particularly pleased to have me at MinLaw, where I was the first ever legally-trained political colleague of his (other than his former "boss", Mr Barker) at the Ministry. Perhaps, that was why I was tasked very early on to undertake a major task that required legal expertise. From December 1993, a small team of officers,[6] chief of whom was Owi Beng Ki from the Attorney-General's Chambers, and I ploughed through all our statutes and subsidiary legislation to determine which among them did not require the involvement of the President. In all, we reviewed 500 provisions and their subsidiary legislation, and submitted our Report in August 1995. Then President Ong Teng Cheong commended the Committee for "doing a most thorough job". When I stepped down, Prof Jaya very kindly said of me, that I was a "very steady and reliable colleague" whom he could turn to for assistance in tackling difficult issues", further adding that he was "very fortunate" to have had me with him at both MHA and MinLaw. He was that kind of a boss — affirming and appreciative.

When Mr Wong Kan Seng took over the helm at MHA in January 1994, with Prof Jaya switching the Foreign Affairs portfolio with him, I also worked very closely with Mr Wong. As a legally-trained colleague, I think I added value to policy discussions with my legal insights. At MHA, there were many more community outreach events, as well as functions that involved thousands of MHA volunteers. Again, with my temperament, I think I fitted in here very nicely, gracing many of these events, setting an easy and informal tone which helped put everyone at ease. The signature events included Traffic Police's annual Road Safety and Courtesy campaign, Year-End Festive Season Crime Prevention roadshow, Civil Defence's annual Civil Defence Day Parade as well as twice-yearly Officers' Commissioning Parades, Community Safety and Security seminars and award ceremonies with stakeholders such as local merchants, Singapore Hotel Association and such, the many Community Engagement outreaches and the Internal Security Department's annual Governmentware ("Govware") seminar, which reached out to trusted infocomm partners in the community to keep Singapore safe and secure. Like in MinLaw, I also immersed myself in MHA's annual staff events that promoted sports and healthy living such as the Home United Sports and Recreation Association (HUSRA) annual Home Team Games.[7] These became "my events" where I was, and gladly so, the "resident" Guest-of-Honour! Other than these regular events, as President of Home Team NS Association (an Association for MHA's "reservists") for 18 years, it was my joy to have interacted with successive batches of very enthusiastic and committed reservists or Operationally-Ready NSmen. Overseas, I attended many of the ASEAN meetings of Interior and Home Affairs Ministers, dubbed the ASEAN Ministerial Meeting on Transnational Crime (AMMTC), and co-chaired a Joint Working Committee with the Qatari Minister in charge of the Interior[8] to advance Singapore–Qatar cooperation on security matters. As office-holder in MHA, I had to be up to speed with issues concerning safety and security, where the quick input of Police was key. Hence, Police saw it fit to designate a senior officer to respond to my queries on all Police-related matters in a timely manner.⁹ At MHA, unlike MinLaw, time was often of the essence in handling many matters that arose. When I retired, MHA's Policy and Operations Department good-humouredly presented me a mug and a T-shirt, each with the word "Survivor" on it!

In terms of personality, I was a good fit to Mr Wong's tough personality. At internal staff meetings, I shared my perspectives and views frankly. Although Mr Wong did not agree with me all the time, I believe I added value in rendering the final version of many of MHA's policies more rounded and compassionate. As Minister, Mr Wong was a good listener, not only to me but to other MHA officers as well. He was a popular boss, heading a tough ministry. Indeed, it is no coincidence that many top civil servants today have done a stint at MHA, a wonderful training ground especially in terms of cultivating an "operational mindset". (I myself was there for 18 years!) For me, it was also great that Prof Jaya and Mr Wong were senior members of the Cabinet who knew and trusted each other and were good friends, as well as "competitive" golfing partners! This made the task of juggling my work commitments between the two ministries that much easier and more manageable. When I stepped down from politics in May 2011, in a heart-warming gesture which is appreciated, Mr Wong shared in his tribute that we had learnt from each other working as a team at MHA, and that Home Team officers would remember me as "approachable, big-hearted and principled". Using a football analogy, he added that I was a "versatile player", whether it was tackling loan sharks, slowing down drug abuse, or grooming younger civil servants.

A lasting memory of how well and closely we worked together was when, early on in my time as office-holder, the three of us, together with DPM Teo Chee Hean, who was then Senior Minister of State for Defence and Acting Minister for the Environment, formed a team to participate in the annual TNP Big Walk on 21 May 1995. As Prof Jaya was the most senior in the group and was team leader, we light-heartedly called ourselves the Jaya Walkers, with the second "a" crossed out; that is, we were the

"Jay-walkers"! We even had a red and white T-shirt with our team name boldly emblazoned on the back! I think the other walkers appreciated our presence in their midst as one of them. The following day, *The New Paper* reported that someone had commented, "Jayá Walkers! Nice name! See also got Johnnie Walkers today or not?" Another quote was "*Garang* (fierce), Jayá Walkers". Our team leader was so serious about us putting up a good show that we even met once early in the morning to practise walking together at the East Coast Parkway! I must say that being an outdoor person, I really enjoyed those outings. The message here is that all leaders, in whatever fields of endeavour, no matter how busy they are, should spend time together playing games (tennis, badminton, futsal or golf) or just exercising (walk, jog or cycle). The bonding among themselves and with the people they work with will prove invaluable. Such informal interaction engenders friendship and trust among co-workers, no matter how high up they may be in the organisational hierarchy.

Recognising that I could continue to play a role at both Ministries after my retirement from politics, especially in tapping the wide network and goodwill garnered with MHA's and MinLaw's many volunteers over the 18 years I was there, I was appointed to helm, on a pro bono basis, several Committees at both Ministries where volunteers play a key role. These were MHA's Home Team Volunteer Network Steering Committee, MinLaw's Advisory Committee on Community Mediation, and the Legal Aid Pro bono Steering Committee.

Indeed, not being in Cabinet, I retained much of my privacy. For example, I did not have a security officer (SO) accompanying me wherever I went. I feel the omnipresence of the SO may act as somewhat of a barrier to the Minister connecting effectively and naturally with the ground. Inadvertently (and probably unintentionally), the Minister tends to act in a more constrained manner. In terms of image, some may feel that he is less accessible as the SOs can appear as a shield. Moreover, there are precious few private moments for him. Psychologically, it may take a toll on him or her. Still, in today's security climate,[10] I suppose such a trade-off is necessary. Hopefully, the day will come when we can adopt a more nuanced risk-based approach, for example, assigning security officers only to key political office-holders such as the Prime Minister, Deputy Prime Ministers, and key Ministers, such as the Home Affairs and Defence Ministers.[11] Alternatively, we could consider reducing the level of security coverage when the Minister is interacting with his own grassroots leaders and residents in familiar settings in his own constituency.[12]

During my time, especially in the earlier years, I felt that Singapore politics tended to be somewhat Minister-centric. With the Ministers expected to take charge of their Ministries, they had to act as though they were very much in charge. There was little room for any perceived sign of softness or uncertainty. While providing leadership was essential, and "the buck" does stop with the Minister, this unwarranted focus on them, unwittingly, I felt, caused some of them to be somewhat stiff and self-conscious occasionally, for example, at meetings or functions. On these occasions, they came across as being overly-officious. Another downside to this was that unless a civil servant was made of strong stuff, knew his subject matter very well, and was prepared to stick his or her neck out, he or she might choose to second-guess the Minister in policy formulation. Thankfully, I did not come across many such officers during my time. I am happy to see that the current crop of Ministers appear much more relaxed and informal when officiating at events. Many of them smile quite a bit more, speaking without notes and "off-the-cuff" on these occasions. Even with a prepared text, some also *ad lib*, expressing their thoughts freely and naturally, which helps them to come across as being more personable. I hope they exercise more flexibility and latitude in running their Ministries too! In today's climate, we do need civil servants, especially those in the senior ranks, made of stern stuff who can hold their own in discussions with the political officer-holders, no doubt respectfully but also honestly. Better policies can then be formulated.

Not being a Cabinet Minister also enabled me to live life as normally as possible. Hence, there were occasions when I attended my children's school concerts or prize-presentation ceremonies when they were young, or fetched them from school events or friends' birthday parties. Other times, I ran family errands such as buying food from nearby Newton Hawker Centre in shorts and T-shirt. I also jogged often at the Botanic Gardens in the evening, refreshed and energised not only by the cool evening air but also by the friendly waves and smiles from fellow joggers. I think this ability to just be myself, and to walk the ground freely and naturally helped me to maintain a better perspective of ground issues as they impacted fellow Singaporeans.

At MHA and MinLaw, I contributed to policy formulation, also helping to promote many of them on the ground. I shared freely with both Prof Jaya and Mr Wong initiatives which I felt should be implemented. These included some of the "second chance and helping" initiatives which are discussed in Chapter 3. These initiatives gave hope to the more vulnerable members of society such as prison inmates (both while they were incarcerated and upon their release), young offenders, mentally-handicapped offenders and recovering drug addicts, as well as those who were down and out, such as undischarged bankrupts or innocent homeowners assailed by loan sharks, and others plagued with relational conflicts with their neighbours. These measures assured them of society's concern for them and its readiness to alleviate their hardship.

At both Ministries, I also looked into the bulk of the appeals received from members of the public and Members of Parliament. It was a heavy load and responsibility (especially at MHA), which I sought to perform diligently and seriously. As in the case of PQs and Bills in Parliament, across ministries, I was probably the office-holder during my time who handled the most appeals! I felt that anyone who made the effort to pen down and send in an appeal to either Ministry or made the effort to see his or her MP at the weekly Meet the People session (who then sent an appeal to me) deserved my fullest attention. I kept a lookout for the deserving cases — those with heart-warming stories to tell — that needed the layers of bureaucracy to be peeled off, and for guidelines and policies to be interpreted compassionately. In this spirit, I dealt with appeals that ranged from traffic offences, applications for permanent residence or long-term visit passes and to be discharged from bankruptcy, to requests to stay longer on state premises. In addition, there were complaints against police, prison, civil defence and immigration officers that had to be looked at carefully, fairly, and judiciously. Of the thousands of appeals that I handled, it is difficult to highlight any, as all were unique, involving individuals whose plights were very real to them. There is really no comparison. However, one case in the early years gives me special satisfaction.

This concerned a family helmed by an elderly matriarch who had probably entered Singapore illegally when she was much younger. No one could verify her status when her case surfaced many years later as she had no papers on her. Going by the book, she and her family should have been required to leave Singapore. However, there was really nowhere we could send them to. So the Immigration and Checkpoint Authority (ICA) issued special passes for them to live here. With the special passes however, it was difficult for the children to study and work here. When this case came to my attention, I felt for the family, especially the innocent children. I worked very hard with officers in the then Immigration Department to facilitate their continued stay here and, more importantly, to enable the children to study and later work here. I am glad that we exercised compassion. In July 1994, I received a letter from them. They shared that they "were stunned on receiving the letter of approval. Our joy is beyond description. You have given us hope, a sense of security and assurance of success in life. We can have peace of mind to make our utmost contribution to the country of Singapore which we love dearly."

Then, in January 1998, I received a note from a kind-hearted Singaporean — a benefactor to the family who had been appealing on their behalf through the years — who gave an update on the family as follows: "The two older children obtained their PR status last year. The youngest son, H, was given a work permit in

November 1997 after completing his NTC2. Now, her three children are gainfully employed. Mdm K would like you to know that she and her family are very grateful to you for solving their problems."

This is just one story. Many stories shared this plea for approval to be granted to a loved one to stay or work in Singapore. Most of them concerned recently-married foreign wives. The Singaporean husband encountered difficulty sponsoring her long-term stay here as he typically either did not work or, more often, did not have a stable income. In handling these appeals, I would exercise as much compassion as I defensibly could, extending the foreign spouse's stay in Singapore so that the family would be kept intact. Hence, I was overjoyed when MHA introduced a Long-Term Visit Pass Plus (LTVP+) — two years or so after I had stepped down from office — that would enable these foreign spouses who had a Singapore Citizen child to enjoy an extended stay of three years, renewable up to five years. It is also good that we have made it easier for stateless persons to live in Singapore, and to study and work here.

It was my privilege and joy to have touched many lives through these appeals.

All in all, it was a great time of learning and of stretching myself during those 18 years at MinLaw and MHA. It would not have been possible for me to have done all that I did at MinLaw and MHA without the excellent support of my two long-standing Personal Assistants, Poh Choo (MHA) and Kamala (MinLaw), who stayed with me throughout my time at both Ministries. Many have provided me feedback that Poh Choo and Kamala were very helpful and courteous. This was especially so when callers were anxious about something, for example, whether I had considered their appeal, had time to consider an invitation to an event, or whether I could shift my schedule around to accommodate an invitation to a function. That cheered me greatly. I think that often how Personal Assistants and Secretaries come across, in a sense, reflect the sort of boss they served. I also received excellent support from my press secretary at MHA,

Gillian Ong, who often worked under pressure of time. All in all, both at MHA and MinLaw, it was my great privilege to have worked with a great team of enthusiastic, committed, and able officers throughout the 18 years I was there. To all of them, I owe a big debt of gratitude.

Lessons in Leadership

1 Empathy and compassion, especially for the more vulnerable in society are the hallmarks of a great society. They are key attributes that any leader must have. These are not just mushy feelings expressed only in words. While words and a gentle touch such as a warm handshake or a pat on the shoulders, when appropriate, do have their place, when the opportunity arises, the concrete expression of empathy and compassion through actions by a leader — such as sending a card to a colleague who is undergoing a crisis or showing up at a wake — can go a long way.

2 In many arenas, leadership can be complex and requires adaptability, flexibility, and versatility. Often, a leader has to interact, lead, and deal with a wide variety of people. Not all leaders are naturally as versatile, as comfortable wearing a suit as a pair of football shorts. Still, you should be mindful that identification with the people you lead and being accepted as "one of the boys" raises their comfort level when you are with them. A sign of bad leadership is when you as the leader are too conscious of your position and seek to put others "on a leash" to reinforce your "higher position"!

3 Teamwork is key to any successful organisation. Knowing your place and how you can add value to organisational objectives are important mindsets to cultivate. I sought to do this as a strong number two in MHA and MinLaw. In this regard, knowing your own strengths as well as the strengths and weaknesses of your colleagues is key. Be clear as to what you can bring to the table. Adapt and fit your contributions in line with the organisational needs and culture.

Endnotes

1. See *TODAY*, 29 October, p. 2.
2. See *The Streats*, "Fighting Chance", 29 October 2001, p. 29.
3. Though not a government scholar, I pursued my Master of Laws at the Harvard Law School on a Loke Foundation scholarship.
4. I cannot now be sure but I think this was one reason why I did not secure a PSC scholarship in 1973 upon completion of my 'A' levels in 1972, where I scored a '1' for the General Paper, 2 'A's and 2 'B's. As far as I know, the top Arts student in that year (1972) scored '1' for GP and had 3 'A's and a 'B'. At that time, most if not all of the PSC scholarships went to students in engineering, medicine, or the sciences.
5. This was the case until Mr Shanmugam became Minister for Law and Second Minister for Home Affairs in 2008.
6. The other key officers involved were Dora Neo, a NUS Law Faculty don who was then on attachment at MinLaw, and P Ramanathan, a long-standing officer at MinLaw.
7. As in MinLaw, I donated a Challenge Shield named the Ho Peng Kee Challenge Trophy to these Games in 2009 for the best-performing Home Team Department. By then, I had graced this annual event no less than 10 times since HUSRA's inception in 1998.
8. He was Sheikh Abdullah Bin Nasser Bin Khalifa Al-Thani, who has now become the Prime Minister.
9. I remain grateful to Ang Hak Seng, who later became Chief Executive of the People's Association, and is now Deputy Secretary at the Ministry of Culture, Community and Youth (MCCY), for his timely and comprehensive input.
10. As recently reminded by the attack on MP Joe Cox in the United Kingdom, politicians do face such danger, any time.
11. If I am not wrong, this is the approach in some countries like the United Kingdom.
12. During these times, a few trusted grassroots leaders, who are suitably trained, can possibly help in this role.

Chapter 3 | MY WORK AT MINLAW AND MHA

The most hopeful strategy for reducing youth crime is to identify the main risks and ways of reducing these within a community, through a concerted and integrated approach. Since 1995, the IMYC has adopted a "many helping hands approach" in dealing with the challenges of youth crime.

My message as Chairman, IMYC in The Right Side: Commemorating A Decade of Partnership to Rebuild Young Lives (2006)

As in battle, even with the best of plans, the commanders have to make constant adjustments to suit changing field circumstances. This was our approach as we constantly scanned the horizon and adapted along the way... When you fight drugs, you have to be very hands-on. To rally the troops, your commitment and enthusiasm must show through. You have to speak from the heart... You have to say what you feel to encourage them to fight, and when that happens — really, the people on the ground will be ready to support you.

My sharing in Slaying the Dragon, Singapore's Fight Against Drugs, 2006

This is a proud moment for you... All of you have been groomed to handle command appointments in the SCDF... The threats we face today arise not just from emergencies like wars or disasters but also from global terrorism. We must continue to be vigilant... As SCDF senior officers, your responsibility is to direct human and physical resources to save lives and protect property... Whilst technology is a vital force multiplier, it is only as effective as the people who operate and command it... You must discharge your responsibilities with dedication, professionalism and honour. The public look up to you to save and protect them in times of need. I am confident that the 26 of you will bear your uniform with pride and make Singapore and the SCDF proud.

Passing Out Parade, 29th SCDF Basic Officers' Course (BOC) on 20 February 2003[1]

We had started to toughen measures against loansharking in 2005. We have been closely monitoring the effect of these enhanced measures... We recognise that we are in a battle of wits with determined loan shark syndicates... Sir, in summary, MHA recognises that loansharking remains a scourge on the ground and will lead collective efforts to tackle it. Let all of us in Singapore declare war against loan sharks!

My response to a PQ in Parliament on 18 August 2009

It would not have been possible without the efforts put in by the NSmen over the years. What we are seeing today is the work of all of us. We have come a long way. From two clubhouses, we have grown to six — with everybody chipping in. It has been a great privilege to work with a group of dedicated NSmen.

At a farewell party HomeTeamNS threw for me on 26 May 2011; extracted from a HomeTeamNS magazine article, July–August 2011 issue

My Work at MinLaw and MHA

"The drug situation has worsened. The situation is dire. I want you to form a Committee to look at how to address the rising numbers."

With this charge from Prof Jaya, I undertook my first major assignment at MHA. That was in August 1993, a month or so after I joined MHA. The backdrop to this charge was that the number of addicts in the Drug Rehabilitation Centres (DRCs) had increased dramatically by 75% over a short six years (1987–1993) from 4,652 to 8,130. The number of addicts arrested had also increased by 51% from 3,132 in 1987 to 4,470 in 1993. I set to work on the task in earnest, tapping the collective wisdom and experience of those who had long before me been battling the scourge in the Ministry, various agencies, and on the ground.

By January 1994, our Report was ready. As Prof Jaya had left MHA by then and was succeeded by Mr Wong Kan Seng, we presented our Report to Mr Wong. To Mr Wong's credit, he recognised the urgency of the situation, even though he had not commissioned the Report. By the time the Committee of Supply debate was held in early March 1994, we were ready to announce our recommendations, all of which the Minister for Home Affairs agreed with. I attribute the seamless manner in which our work transcended the succession of Ministers to the excellent relationship and understanding that Prof Jaya and Mr Wong had. As very senior Ministers in the Cabinet, they knew time was of the essence. They were right.

Having spent two years in the backbench and established a public persona as someone who was passionate about giving a second chance to members of our society who were "down and out", I tapped on the network of "friends" I had already established. Thankfully, I did not have to start on a blank page. There were existing programmes and actions on the part of relevant agencies such as the Central Narcotics Bureau, Singapore Police Force (SPF), Singapore Prisons Service (SPS), Halfway Houses, and

Singapore Anti-Narcotics Association (SANA). What was absent was an overriding sense of collective purpose and mission, as well as proper coordination of efforts and integration of programmes. I also had a great advantage in that for several years before entering politics, I was involved in helping recovering drug addicts from one of Singapore's earliest Halfway Houses, the House of Hope. Their residents worshipped in my church as part of their recovery process. I was keenly aware of the unrealised potential that Halfway Houses held out.

This is a good example of how lessons and experiences from an earlier phase of life helped to address issues that I later handled while in political office. I have already highlighted this point in Chapter 1, referring to my on-the-ground outreach in Nee Soon East, where my earlier active days as a student, university don, and hall resident fellow/master had honed my people skills to help me better connect with my residents. Later, I will mention other examples, such as the collective fight against youth crime, advocacy of alternative dispute settlement processes such as arbitration and mediation at MinLaw, being patron of the Children's Cancer Foundation, and being President of the Football Association of Singapore as other examples where earlier experiences and lessons learnt in life helped me to become a better politician and leader. In truth, I see life as a continuum lived out in phases, with each phase shaping and preparing us for later challenges that we face. The thing to do is to live each phase to the fullest. Yes, *carpe diem* indeed!

The master plan which the "Committee to Improve the Drug Situation in Singapore" devised, for many years thereafter, formed the basis of Singapore's fight against drug abuse.[2] The Report signified renewed political will and triggered fresh resolve on all fronts to tackle the then worsening situation. In my experience, it is very important to first signal political will when embarking on a major national exercise, such as recharting our fight against drug-abuse or youth crime, or promoting active aging or sports as a way of life, or galvanising the ground to counter terrorism. This is not to say, however, that in every situation, advocating for good causes must spring from the government. There are examples where citizen-initiated actions have led Government to rethink its position on policies. An early episode is regarding Chek Jawa on Pulau Ubin. Where Government does chart the general direction, it must then involve all relevant stakeholders in the private sector including grassroots bodies, community and relevant voluntary welfare organisations (VWOs), corporations and individual Singaporeans. There is a lot of expertise, experience and passion on the ground that can be tapped! This is something I have been doing over 18 years in political office, and still continue to do now as volunteer chairman of the Home Team Volunteer Network (HTVN) Steering Committee, interacting with close to 20,000 active volunteers.

The master plan drew up a slew of measures in four areas: firstly, preventive drug education (PDE); secondly, enforcement; thirdly, treatment and rehabilitation; and fourthly, aftercare and continued rehabilitation. To ensure proper coordination of these measures, a lead agency was appointed in each of the four areas to ensure synergy and continuity. I saw our fight against the drug scourge as a continuum, a seamless fight. Any gap would disrupt our overall efforts; for example, if drug addicts who had completed their term in our drug rehabilitation centres were not effectively rehabilitated upon their release, they would return to their old ways. Worse, they would have made new 'friends' while incarcerated, thus widening their sphere of influence upon release. Likewise, even if some were successfully rehabilitated, unless we were successful in stemming the inflow of new addicts, the fight would be interminable and relentless!

CNB led in PDE and Enforcement; the Prisons Service in Treatment and Rehabilitation and the Singapore Corporation in Rehabilitation, and Aftercare (SCORE) in Aftercare and Continued Rehabilitation. For aftercare and rehabilitation, to me, it was important that Government fully engaged and tapped existing strength in the community, especially that of the halfway houses, as most if not all were run by ex-addicts, some of whom were role models for struggling addicts. Tapping into my networks in the halfway houses arising from my past experience in The House of Hope, I rallied them and secured their firm commitment to do their part. A scheme was implemented whereby some financial assistance was extended to them based on the number of ex-addicts they brought under their wings. Government also did more to help them with securing or extending the use of premises. What is pivotal was that for the first time, Government acknowledged that religion had a key part to play in getting drug addicts to turn over a new leaf. Thus, we ensured that there were Christian, Muslim, Hindu and Buddhist halfway houses, and even started a secular halfway house for those who were atheists or agnostics. In this way, the important work done by the halfway houses through the years was recognised and acknowledged. In turn, this encouraged many of their benefactors, especially the churches, temples, and mosques, to do even more. There was a positive knock-on effect.

In the same spirit of engaging and tapping latent strength in the community, the National Council Against Drug Abuse (NCADA) was formed in January 1995 to spearhead PDE; the Community Action for the Rehabilitation of Ex-Offenders (CARE) Network formed in 2000 to coordinate the work of all the aftercare agencies and the Yellow Ribbon Project was launched in 2004 to garner wider community support for the fight against the drug scourge, especially employers and the families of prisoners and addicts.[3] I was closely involved in all three initiatives.

Indeed, securing community support in our fight was essential. Thus, over the years, I attended many events, meetings, and functions to rally the ground. At the outset, we knew that we had to put the onus squarely at the feet of the drug addict himself. Hitherto, there were some people whose sympathies lay with the addict. These people viewed drug addiction as more of a medical problem. The Committee felt that if we were to effectively help those who were sincere in their desire to turn over a new leaf, it was critical to secure the community's buy-in. Thus, the key was to impress upon the addicts that they had no one but themselves to blame for their predicament, and to help them realise that their actions impacted not only themselves but their loved ones as well. Once there was open acknowledgment of wrongdoing and a clear expression of a desire to change, community compassion and action could kick in. Moreover, we decided early on that we should not "pussyfoot" on what was clear at that time, that is, the large majority of addicts came from the Malay community. Although this was a widely-known fact, especially among those familiar with the ground situation, it was never openly acknowledged. Thus, while the Malay community leaders and VWOs extended their help to the fight, it was not a strong, focused and directed effort. Only when the Government came out with the facts and rallied the Malay leaders and community did the efforts become more focused and concerted. A few years later, when we toughened the penalties against third-time drug offenders, including meting out caning and long-term detention against them,[4] as we had worked with the community and won their support, there was no public outcry against these tougher measures. With our earlier efforts in place, the community also appreciated that our approach was a balanced one. There were both tough as well as "soft" or helping measures such as greater halfway house support for first- and second-time addicts sent to a drug rehabilitation centre.

Working together, we turned the tide. The DRC population peaked at 8,700 in 1994, but declined by 30% to 6,160 in 1997. On the aftercare front, the relapse rate (calculated based on those who were re-arrested for drug consumption within a two-year period) declined from a high of 81.2% in 1994 to 65.9% in 1997. By October 2015, the relapse rate had dropped to about 27%, which is very good by global standards.

This was a key area where I sought to provide a "second chance" to those who had strayed but were sincere in turning over a new leaf. Looking back, providing second chances was a common thread that weaved through quite a bit of my work in my years in politics. Hence, I was dubbed the "second chance" man!

Addressing Juvenile Delinquency and Youth Crime

I was privileged to have led another inter-Ministry and inter-agency effort, also for about 15 years, this time against youth crime. I was appointed chairman of the Inter-Ministry Committee against Juvenile Delinquency (IMJD) in 1995 when a national-level committee chaired by then Minister for Community Development Abdullah Tarmugi to look into the phenomena of dysfunctional families, juvenile delinquency, and drug abuse recommended the formation of such a committee. The IMJD drew members from relevant Ministries such as MHA, MinLaw, MOE, and the Ministry of Community Development (MCD), as well as key agencies such as the Attorney-General's Chambers (AGC), the then Subordinate Courts, the National Council of Social Service (NCSS), Singapore Prison Service (SPS) and Singapore Police Force (SPF). Later, we also had a representative from the Institute of Technical Education. It also had academics from the local universities who contributed significantly to our cause. They were Dr S Vasoo (then MP for Tanjong Pagar GRC) from the National University of Singapore, and Dr Alfred Choi from Nanyang Technological University. Other pioneer longstanding Committee members were Ang Bee Lian from the then Ministry of Community Development, Tina Hung from NCSS, and Eric Low who was then Vice-Chairman of the National Crime Prevention Council. Youth crime trends in the early 1990s had sounded alarm bells ringing. Arrest of young Singaporeans, that is, offenders between seven and 15 years of age, nearly doubled over 10 years, from 691 in 1980 to 1,205 in 1990. This rose a further 74.4% to 2,102 in 1994, which represented an annual increase of 8.3% over a 15-year period. As in the case of our fight against drug abuse, I seized the opportunity to shape developments in this critical area and ran with the ball, ably supported once again by a team of civil servants and volunteers, all of whom believed sincerely in the cause of nurturing youth potential and giving wayward youths a second chance. I continued to chair this inter-Ministry committee until I retired from politics in May 2011.[5]

My earlier experiences had prepared me to lead our fight against youth crime. I was a very active student at the Anglo-Chinese School, National Junior College, and the Law Faculty at the Singapore University. I had attended a local University and completed two and half years of national service, just like other Singaporean boys. Having spent 12 years as a resident fellow and Master of a very active university student hall of residence, five eventful years as the Sub-Dean and then Vice-Dean at the Law Faculty, NUS where one of my key roles was to interface with the students and their elected leaders, and five fulfilling years as Chairman of the National Police Cadet Corps Council (NPCC) from 1988 to 1993, I had accumulated valuable ground experience working with young people. In my time at the Law Faculty (the last two of which were as a backbencher in Parliament) and as NPCC Council Chairman, I had nurtured many friendships and contacts at the various Ministries including the Ministry of Education and Ministry of Community Development, two key partners of the IMJD. I also knew many of the Court officers including then Senior District Judge Richard Magnus, who had provided inspirational leadership over more than 15 years at the Subordinate Courts. SDJ Magnus' initiatives provided impetus to many of IMJD's earlier initiatives. In addition, I had taught many students at the Law Faculty, some of whom later made significant contributions to our work at IMJD. Special mention must be made of Mark Tay and May Mesenas, two IMJD members who were then Juvenile Court Judges, and Bala Reddy, who was then Deputy Public Prosecutor at the AGC. This is one example where my varied background and network of contacts stood me in good stead in my work at MHA and MinLaw.

Indeed, the Committee acted vigorously to tackle youth crime, introducing more than 30 initiatives. Many of these were groundbreaking. They straddled different Ministries where close collaboration was key. In this way, we all worked closely together in an informal manner, bonded by our strong desire to steer every potential youth offender away from trouble, and to rehabilitate every youth offender who sincerely wished to reform. We were friends and comrades championing a common cause, and not committee members nominated by our bosses to just do a job. Our meetings were free-flowing and invigorating, with everyone chipping in without inhibition. I judiciously avoided a "Minister-centric" approach, that is, one where the Minister dominates discussion. Indeed, I do not recall us reporting to any Minister, even though the Committee was set up by the Minister for Community Development. We met once every three months or so, and operated largely on our own steam, supported magnificently by very motivated officers at the National Youth Council (NYC), which acted as the Committee's secretariat. These included successive NYC Directors such as Lee How Sheng, Foong Hin Cheong, Ng How Yue, and Goh Chye Boon. Karen Lee was a key NYC staff who played a key role in implementing many of our initiatives over the years.

The work of the Committee and the recognition it has received from both local and foreign quarters are well-documented.[6] Its initiatives included diversionary programmes such as the Guidance programme[7] and the Streetwise programme;[8] educational outreaches such as Project CRuSH[9] and School Roadshows;[10] programmes to "inoculate" the wider student problem from going down the slippery slope, such as a National Mentoring Network[11] and a Prison Visit Programme,[12] and schemes geared towards improving the disciplinary tone of our schools such as the Honorary VSC scheme[13] and Peer Mediation Support scheme.[14] These outreach efforts, programmes, and schemes reduced youth crime considerably between 1997 and 2001 (from 4,412 arrests to 2,756 arrests) before increasing in line with overall crime trends to 5,050 in 2005. Thereafter, it trended downwards again, with 4,174 arrests in 2010, 3,477 arrests in 2011 and 3,120 arrests in 2014.[15] In the later years of my chairmanship of the Committee, we began to focus more on upstream issues. For example, we looked more closely at studies to better understand the phenomenon of youth crime; we got agencies talking on how they could share data more effectively without breaching any confidence; and we undertook a study to consider the different pathways by which youths could fall into crime and how we could prevent that. Then Parliamentary Secretary for National Development Maliki Osman who was Vice-Chairman of the Committee led a study which produced a very useful report in June 2010 titled "Youth Crime Indicators Taskforce Report".[16]

Community-Based Sentences and Offenders with Mental Disability

In the many national efforts that I was involved in, engaging the community was critical in ensuring their success. These included campaigns to improve road safety, tackle youth crime, reduce drug abuse, counter terrorism, reduce rubbish chute fires, and promote community mediation. While these causes lent themselves readily to securing the community's support, enthusing Singaporeans to accept the prospect of having convicted prisoners in their midst was a more daunting prospect. However, with the introduction and enhancement of community-based sentences, we crossed that rubicon, much to the credit of Singaporeans.

The first set of community-based sentences was introduced in 2000, following the adoption of recommendations made by the Committee on Community-based Sentences which I chaired. This groundbreaking scheme enabled first-time inmates of minor offences to return home towards the tail-end of their sentence, thus enabling them to work and receive family support. We treaded carefully before going ahead with implementing the scheme as, in effect, we were releasing offenders out of prison earlier than the period meted out by the court.[17] Should any of these released inmates commit a serious crime during this period of early release, that would likely lead to a public outcry! Still, we bit the bullet and proceeded. The scheme proved successful and was expanded in 2004.

From May 2000 to June 2004, about 4,100 inmates were emplaced on home detention, and 99.3% completed their prison term while out of prison without relapsing to crime. Only 30 failed to complete the programme.[18] The criteria for qualifying under the scheme was then expanded to offences where the sentence was not less than four weeks (from not less than six months) and the maximum home detention emplacement period was increased from six to 12 months. The range of offences that qualified for the scheme was also expanded. Since then, many more inmates have benefited from the scheme.

When the Committee was reconvened in 2006, its deliberations led to the introduction of another set of innovative community-based sentences. These included the Mandatory Treatment Order (MTO) which could be invoked if the criminal act was due to a treatable psychological cause or condition such as schizophrenia. This way, an offender with mental disability would not be subject to the rigours of incarceration, and instead would benefit from a medical regime imposed by the Institute of Mental Health (IMH). As treatment could be costly, we rallied the medical professionals to chip in and to do their part. To its credit, the Anglican Church of Singapore responded magnificently, setting up a Community Rehabilitation and Support Service in 2006 which launched two new centres in Pasir Ris and Yishun in 2011. The Singapore Anglican Community Services till today remain champions and a much appreciated partner in this key outreach.[19] A second innovative measure was the Short Detention Order (SDO), which could be invoked if a first-time offender commits a minor offence which ordinarily would attract a prison term. This Order puts the offender behind bars for a short period (up to two weeks or so, but normally would be less), which would not count as a prison record. Spending a limited time in prison prevented contamination as he would not be interacting with hardened criminals, yet it enabled him to reflect on his wrongdoing, and very importantly, he could keep his job. A third measure was the Day Reporting Order (DRO), spanning three to 12 months, which required an offender to report on a regular basis at a Day Reporting Centre which would be conveniently located. Counselling could then be carried out at that time. It also enabled a counsellor to monitor the offender's progress in rehabilitation. Community Works Orders (CWO)[20] — which I felt at that time could possibly be adapted to enable Traffic Police to require traffic offenders to distribute pamphlets on safe driving at public places including outside pubs for drink-drivers — and possible wider use of Community Service Orders (CSO) for adults were other key measures introduced.

These measures gave the Courts greater flexibility in deciding on the appropriate punishment in any particular case. More importantly, the Courts could require an offender to undergo a combination of orders, for example, a five-day short detention order followed by weekly visits to a Day Reporting Centre over a three-month period. For good measure, if the wrongful behaviour warranted it, a community work order or Community Service Order (CSO) could be further imposed to imbue positive values and behaviour in the offender. These measures *in toto* made for a fuller and rounder penal regime where the punishment meted out could cater to the offender's needs, especially from the viewpoint of reforming him. The new community-based sentences came into effect in January 2011, when amendments to the Criminal Procedure Code became operational. Instead of incarceration, offenders of less serious offences, especially those involving offenders with mental disability, were brought before the Community Court which meted out community-based sentences, as appropriate. The SPS' 2011 annual report reported that the number of prison inmates fell by 10.1% from 11,154 inmates to 10,028 inmates, with lawyers and prison counsellors attributing this fall in numbers to the Courts' positive adoption of the community-based sentences.[21] By May 2013, it was reported that more than 100 offenders had been placed on the Day Reporting Order and the Community Service Order since their introduction with a completion rate of above 90%.[22] In his 2016 Opening of the Legal Year speech, then Attorney-General VK Rajah said that AGC would be considering all possible options such as community sentences for less serious offences. This is good news.

Another set of measures which I worked on arose from recommendations made by an Inter-Ministry Committee on Offenders with Mental Disabilities. I had chaired this Committee with members from AGC, the then Subordinate Courts, the then Ministry of Community Development, Youth and Sports (MCYS), Ministry of Health (MOH), MHA, the SPF and SPS. We submitted our Report in August 2006. One outcome was greater sensitivity in handling suspects with such disabilities. In this regard, I am again cheered that there is now greater awareness of this growing problem in our midst; for example, in late 2011, the Institute of Mental Health released the results of a nationwide survey involving more than 6,500 respondents, which revealed that the top three most prevalent mental conditions were major depressive disorder, alcohol abuse and obsessive compulsive disorder. Of concern was that it took, on average, four years for someone suffering from depression to seek help.[23] In addition, the MOH announced in March 2012 that a key part of its Health Masterplan was to deliver care more effectively, by having more people treated in the community rather than in hospitals.[24] This was something the Committee felt was important, that is, for the community including volunteer healthcare professionals, to take ownership and cognizance of the problem.

For a start, the Committee emphasised the importance of widening the use of the Development Disability Registry, to cover as many people with mental disabilities as possible. Police also improved its Standard Operating Procedures (SOP) for the conduct of interviews to include checking this Registry when a suspect was suspected of having mental disability. In addition, we advocated for some sort of identification tag or card to be carried by these people so that should they be picked up by Police for any reason, their disability would immediately be made known. Further, Police worked with several VWOs to enlist their help to be on standby to assist police with interviewing anyone suspected or identified with mental disability. I was therefore happy to read what then Attorney-General Sundaresh Menon said, in January 2012 in his Opening of the Legal Year speech, that a Committee had been formed to study whether there was a need to enact legislation that would further strengthen these processes and enact them as law. In particular, he shared that a screening test, to help Police identify individuals with mental disabilities before they were put through interviews as suspects, victims or witnesses was being considered. All these efforts culminated in the launch of the Appropriate Adult Scheme in April 2015. Administered by the Law Society's Pro Bono Services Office, trained volunteers are deployed to accompany suspects with mental disability when they are interviewed by Police.[25]

Other than early identification, the Committee's work led to the introduction of a diversion programme for intellectually disabled offenders, that is, those with low IQs, modelled after the Guidance programme initiated by the IMJD. As in the Guidance programme, offenders were issued with a stern warning instead of being prosecuted upon successful completion of a six-month programme. By 2011, about 10 of such offenders had benefited from this diversion programme.

Another important focus involved dealing with inmates with mental disorder. The Committee recognised that, on average, about five to 10% of any prison population would suffer from one form of mental disorder or another. These included schizophrenia, stress reaction, depression, and adjustment order. These conditions made them unsuitable to be in the mainstream inmate population. While they were not serious enough to be isolated in the Prison Psychiatric Unit, we felt that these offenders should be segregated, both for their own sake as well as to free up resources and energy of the prison staff so that they could concentrate on reforming the inmate population at large. Removing them from the mainstream inmate population also meant that they would not disrupt the other inmates' routine as much, as when they flared up. The Committee deliberated on this approach for some time, recognising that it would be resource- and labour-intensive. There would be need for a strong corps of medical personnel as well as recurrent costs. Thankfully, we succeeded in tapping on the Reinvestment Fund to launch the programme, initially on a small scale. Over time, this programme was scaled up, and it now operates out of one of Changi Prison's clusters as a dedicated Housing unit catering to inmates with mental problems, as diagnosed by doctors from the Institute of Mental Health. At any one time, I understand that there are about 150 inmates in this facility. These inmates are prescribed medication and undergo specialised counselling sessions to stabilise their condition. While the Anglican Church has provided yeomen service to these inmates when they leave prison, it is my hope that more community resources can be tapped into, along similar lines such as the collaborative scheme between the Law Society of Singapore and the Singapore Psychiatric Association for the assessment of accused persons exhibiting symptoms of mental illness (mentioned above). This is important not only from the resources-utilisation viewpoint but also from the viewpoint of continuity in treatment of these identified inmates when they are released.

Protocols on Helping Abused Spouses, Spent Regime, Composition Fines, Debt Repayment Schemes

As Parliamentary Secretary early on in 1994, I had a few memorable exchanges with Nominated MP Kanwaljit Soin who was passionate about and argued for more to be done to protect abused spouses, particularly wives. Although sympathetic, my approach was to explain that Police operated under severe manpower constraints. While there were certainly some cases for Police to intervene immediately upon notification, for example, via a "999" call that a wife was being beaten up, the large majority of cases did not require immediate police intervention. These were cases where an abused wife goes to a police station or police post to make a report after the event. In Chapter 4, I recall one of my early anxious moments as office-holder when I was misunderstood. This arose from the way my parliamentary reply to Dr Soin was reported in the media. That was a useful learning point. A positive outcome from our debates on this issue was that I worked closely with then MHA Deputy Secretary, Lim Soo Peng, to fine-tune police procedures on helping these abused spouses. This included, for example, a revised form which Police, upon a report being lodged, would hand to the victim, explaining to her how she could fill it up and then seek medical treatment at the nearest hospital. In addition, if the victim agreed to the suggestion, she would be put in touch with a voluntary welfare organisation specialising in the field for counselling and support. These moves made it easier for the victim to obtain a Personal Protection Order. The Singapore Council of Women's Organisations (SCWO) also gave its input as to how Police officers could be more effectively trained to handle these cases. I recall this early episode with much satisfaction as our efforts alleviated the plight of this needy group of people in a real way.

Another group of needy people who benefited from another scheme that I was involved in were criminals with records of having committed minor offences. In 2005, MHA amended the law to provide for criminal records of minor offences[26] to be "rendered spent" after a period of three years, if the offender did not re-offend. In effect, the beneficiary of this scheme could reply "No" to a question from a prospective employer if he had a criminal record. As the record was considered "spent", it would not be reflected in the records any longer. To make it easier for an ex-offender to check his or her eligibility under this scheme, Police set up an electronic portal in May 2006 to facilitate these checks — quickly, accurately, and confidentially. The scheme came into effect in October 2005. By 31 March 2007, about 125,000 ex-offenders had benefited from it. Following feedback, both in and out of Parliament, that the scheme would be more effective if employers asked whether a prospective employee had a criminal record (at the time of application), rather than if he had ever been convicted by a court of law (which was the more common question asked then by employers), MHA spearheaded a public education campaign, working with both the Public Service Division (for public servants) and the Singapore Employers' Federation (for private sector employees) to encourage employers to amend their application forms accordingly. These efforts underscored our desire to maximise the positive impact of our "second chance" initiatives.

Indeed, an early effort which resulted in our penal system becoming more rounded was one at MinLaw where, together with officers from MinLaw and AGC,[27] we combed through our legislation to assess which offences which were subject to criminal penalties such as fines and imprisonment could be punished with non-criminal sanctions such as the issuance of warning, offering of composition fines (not counted as a conviction, unlike court fines), imposing of financial penalties, and suspension of licenses and permits. This was a detailed, painstaking effort that took over two years, but at the end of it, proved very worthwhile. For example, some regulatory offences were made compoundable whereas previously they were not. We went further to decriminalise some minor offences, such as the failure to inform the Registrar of Nurses of a change in address or other particulars[28] where instead of criminal prosecution, the Nursing Board could instead censure, suspend, or revoke the licence or impose a financial penalty.

At MinLaw, we introduced a debt repayment scheme (DRS) that ameliorated the hardship suffered by Singaporeans who were in dire financial straits. I had steered its introduction through Parliament. Under it, when considering a bankruptcy application involving a debtor whose personal debts did not exceed $100,000 and who had a regular income, a Court could adjourn the application for up to six months and refer the case to the Official Assignee to enable the debtor to work out a repayment plan. By avoiding bankruptcy, the debtor could keep his job and apportion part of his salary towards repaying the debt. The intention was that the creditor would receive no less than what he would have received if the debtor had gone into bankruptcy, thus achieving a win-win outcome. Other than the DRS, we also introduced an alternative to a court discharge for bankrupts, that is, discharge by the Official Assignee which was more expeditious and certain. Over the years, building on these foundations, successive Ministers have further refined our bankruptcy regime to achieve a better balance between recognising the legitimate interests of a bankrupt (especially one whose bankruptcy arose from business failure) and protecting society at large.

Promoting Alternative Dispute Resolution Processes

A major preoccupation for me at MinLaw was to oversee the development of Alternative Dispute Resolution (ADR) processes.

Sometime in 1996, I shared with Prof Jaya that I felt the time was right to give the growth of ADR in Singapore a boost. Early steps had been made by other institutions such as the then Subordinate Courts (especially in the area of mediation), Singapore International Arbitration Centre (SIAC) (in international arbitration), and the Singapore Institute of Arbitrators (in domestic arbitration). However, I felt that much more could be done and that MinLaw should lead the way. My interest in ADR arose early on when I took a course in International Commercial Arbitration with Professor von Mehren as part of my LL.M. studies at Harvard Law School in 1980–1981. I wrote my requisite LL.M. paper in that course. When I returned to the Law Faculty at the National University of Singapore in 1981, I pursued my interest in ADR; for example, I authored the Singapore chapter in Commercial Arbitration Laws in Asia and the Pacific (1987).[29] I also wrote a few articles on the Small Claims Tribunals Act, then a new initiative here. There was a convergence of interests as I felt it was critical for Singapore to actively nurture a strong ADR culture and framework in Singapore. Prof Jaya once again graciously encouraged me to proceed and to look into the matter.

As in our fight against drugs and youth crime, once again, I first pulled together the strands of work that were already in place. I felt we needed to form a matrix of complementary and mutually-reinforcing measures, with Government giving impetus to the process. Thus, with Prof Jaya's blessings — yes, you guessed right — I formed an inter-ministry and inter-agency committee named the Committee on Alternative Dispute Resolution. Other than the Ministries of Law, Home Affairs, and MCYS, other agencies such as the Subordinate Courts, AGC, NUS, SIAC, and the Law Society were also represented on it. Together, we produced a Report in July 1997 that surveyed the landscape on various ADR processes in general (including arbitration which the Committee noted was fairly well-developed by then) but that focused principally on mediation. In particular, we highlighted the pioneering efforts of the Singapore Academy of Law in proposing the setting up of a Commercial Mediation Centre (which the Committee fully supported), and recommended the setting up of a network of Community Mediation Centres (CMCs) to resolve relational disputes on the ground, such as between neighbours, amicably and efficiently. The Government accepted these recommendations. Prof Jaya in his response said that "the Committee has done a comprehensive study and made recommendations that are practical and relevant to our society".

To operationalise the CMCs, I moved a Bill in Parliament in January 1998 to set up the legal framework. Today, the CMCs[30] have become very much a part of our legal landscape, helping to nurture a society that is less litigious (especially in relation to relational disputes) and promoting stronger neighbourliness and the *kampong* spirit on the ground. In all, CMCs over 18 years of operation have mediated in about 7,500 disputes with a 75% settlement rate. As important as these statistics are, what is really heartwarming are the many hours of willing ears and hearts that about 120 voluntary mediators as peacemakers have put in. In addition, the Annual Youth Mediation Forum, which reached out to schools,[31] enabled our students to better appreciate the value of mediating disputes among themselves. The hope was that as more of our young people became aware of what mediation could do, over time, it would result in a more harmonious Singapore. To ensure that ADR remained firmly on the Ministry's radar, the Committee's proposal that an ADR Division should be formed was also quickly implemented. On this, I must acknowledge the determined contribution of then Deputy Secretary of MinLaw, Lau Wah Ming, who co-laboured with me arduously to put community mediation in Singapore on a strong footing. Other key collaborators were Professor Lim Lan Yuan, a pioneer in Community Mediation who took on a lot of the training of the early batches of mediators (and continues to do so even today) and Gloria Lim, a younger MinLaw staff, who efficiently executed many of our policy decisions on the ground. Till today, I remain involved in community mediation, chairing an Advisory Committee on Community Mediation at MinLaw.

Other than community mediation centres, another key product of the Report was the formation of an ADR Resource Panel which promoted the use of mediation in a wide variety of settings. This Panel drew input from members from a variety of backgrounds. They included mediators, lawyers, academics, arbitral and mediation institution representatives, community leaders who were mediators, the Courts, and the relevant Ministries. The Committee offered a ready platform for practitioners of mediation in diverse areas such as consumer contracts, small commercial claims, banking and insurance, construction, family, surveying and valuing as well as real estate to share ideas and experiences. I understand that lay and industry leaders on the committee appreciated this forum that enabled them to interact with Government. The momentum created has continued; for example, the Ministry of Manpower introduced a tripartite mediation scheme to help junior-level and mid-level professionals, managers and executives (PMETs) settle their disputes in February 2011. The Singapore Mediation Centre has rolled out strategic initiatives such as Singapore Mediation Charter scheme,[32] neutral evaluation service, and several industry-specific schemes.[33] In July 2004, the Resource Panel evolved into an Advisory Committee. The Committee embraced wider terms of reference to focus on developing other ADR processes besides mediation, a key focus of which was arbitration. Its membership was also widened to include more practitioners from established local ADR institutions.[34] A key event organised by the ADR Committee was a National ADR Forum in January 2005 which gave our national ADR efforts a boost. Other issues discussed included the setting up of an ADR website and promoting ADR education in the tertiary institutions. On this front, too, I am happy to see recent efforts to build Singapore up as an ADR hub.

Separately, I worked closely with Prof Jaya to revamp the Singapore International Arbitration Centre. SIAC was chaired by former AG Tan Boon Teik, with Professor Lawrence Boo as CEO, when it was set up in 1991 under the auspices of the Trade Development Board (TDB), and Economic Development Board (EDB). In 1999, the oversight of SIAC was transferred from TDB and EDB to the Singapore Academy of Law and a new Chairman, retired High Court Judge Warren Khoo was appointed. The consensus was that while SIAC had built strong foundations, it needed a boost to bring it to the next level. Under its then

Executive Director, Ang Yong Tong, SIAC successfully raised its profile albeit in a limited way, especially in China. However, we knew that more had to be done to enhance SIAC's overall reputation among arbitration practitioners, not only in China but in the region and in India as well. Thus, the oversight of SIAC was transferred from the SAL to the Singapore Business Federation (SBF) in April 2003, to inject greater commercial acumen into SIAC's marketing and outreach efforts. With the active support of SBF's chairman, Stephen Lee, SIAC received a new lease of life, especially in marketing its services to the international business and legal communities. In May 2004, Warren Khoo stepped down as SIAC chairman. The new chairman was another retired High Court Judge, Goh Joon Seng. At the same time, the former CEO, Professor Lawrence Boo returned to the fold, this time as Deputy Chairman, to help drive SIAC. A new Board of Directors was also installed. In all, it took some effort on the part of Lau Wah Ming and me to steer the strengthening of SIAC through this crucial two- to three-year period. Two persons who played important behind-the-scene roles were Serene Wee, the longstanding CEO of the Singapore Academy of Law, and David Chin from the Trade Development Board and later, the Singapore Business Federation.

With renewed vigour, the new team promoted SIAC, garnering greater success. By July 2008, we had improved the overall tone of arbitration in Singapore with measures such as tax incentives (abolishing withholding tax for foreign arbitrators) and the streamlining of the work pass application for foreign arbitrators and counsel (they were included in the Manpower Ministry's Work-pass Exemption program). In addition, reputed foreign arbitral bodies such as the American Arbitration Association, the International Chamber of Commerce and the Permanent Court of Arbitration were courted to establish a presence in Singapore. In addition, the International Arbitration Act was amended to render it more arbitration-friendly. We continued to fly SIAC and Singapore's flag in a targeted way; for example, I led a delegation to a conference on the "Resolution of Construction Disputes in Asia", jointly organised by SIAC and the Construction Industry

Arbitration Association, India in November 2006. Then Indian President, the late Dr Abdul Kalam, and I spoke at the Conference. SIAC hosted high-profile conferences and seminars, such as the Uncitral 25th anniversary Contracts for International Sale of Goods and 20th Model Arbitration Law Conference, in Singapore in 2005. Today, the SIAC receives many accolades and is widely recognised as a leading centre of arbitration in the region. Still, the success of SIAC, often associated with the opening of the Maxwell Chambers[35] and the appointment of a new Board comprising internationally-renowned arbitration practitioners with diverse backgrounds, headed by Professor Michael Pryles in March 2009, is founded on a very solid foundation laid by previous "contributors to the cause". In particular, we moved with some dexterity in the early years to get the structure right and to put the people to lead in place. Indeed, as early as 2007/2008, an ICC International Court of Arbitration report already ranked Singapore as the top city in Asia for ICC arbitration. With the momentum created, total quantum of claims handled by SIAC soared from $504 million in 2007 to $1.5 billion in 2008. By 2010, a global survey of corporate arbitration users ranked Singapore equally with Paris and Tokyo as a preferred venue for settling disputes.[36] The number of new cases increased steadily over the years from 64 in 2001 to 78 in 2004 to 99 in 2008, then increased exponentially to 160 in 2009 and 198 in 2010, and 222 new cases were filed in 2014 and 271 cases in 2015.[37]

Singapore should press on resolutely to becoming the ADR hub of Asia, not only in terms of the effective settlement of disputes but also in terms of training and thought-leadership. In this regard, recent initiatives such as the Singapore International Mediation Centre (SIMC), the Singapore International Mediation Institute (SIMI), and the Singapore International Dispute Resolution Academy (SIDRA) are steps in the right direction.

Other Major Concerns

I was always kept busy at MHA and MinLaw. A focus common to both Ministries was tackling loan sharks. The phenomenon of loansharking first appeared on MHA's radar screen around 2005. By then, the number of harassment cases had increased significantly.[38] Interestingly, I was given the privilege of leading this fight on both fronts at MHA and MinLaw. At MHA, our key concern was that innocent HDB homeowners were being harassed with increasing ferocity by unscrupulous loansharks and their runners. Not only was paint being splashed on their door, or the heads of pigs being placed outside, shoes and other things on racks were being set on fire as well. Innocent neighbours were not spared. Even cars in adjacent carparks were set on fire. I felt for those who were at the receiving end of these wanton attacks. At MinLaw, we liberalised the regime governing licensed moneylenders. I saw this as complementary to what we were doing at MHA. With greater access to licensed moneylenders, for some, the need to turn to loansharks was diminished. Nevertheless, with greater liberalisation, I was mindful that there was a need to closely monitor the practices of these licensed moneylenders, some of whom were emboldened by the liberalisation. Also, the liberalisation attracted new entrants who were less scrupulous at best, and shady at worse. We had detected practices such as deducting the first repayment upfront upon extension of the loan.[39] I moved two key sets of amendments to the Moneylenders Act in Parliament[40] to strengthen it. I also responded to many PQs on loansharking in Parliament. In one such response, I made a speech declaring "war" on loan sharks. Though stark and dramatic, I felt it was necessary to make this clarion call to rally all stakeholders to greater effort. The downside was that it painted a bleak picture of the loansharking situation in Singapore, worse than it actually was. After all, a war was being declared! In truth, while the situation was dire and not pretty, it was not quite like some countries where gang warfare violence spilled onto the streets. Indeed, a foreign media painted it as such! However, I felt that to rally and galvanise everyone to intensive action, it was necessary to jolt them and grab their attention in a dramatic fashion. Looking back, that was the right thing to do. With collective action, especially the ground actions led by committed grassroots volunteers (and roping in foreign workers as well), the loansharking situation in Singapore has improved very significantly.

On this front, as in many other areas I worked on, it was really good to see so many grassroots groups and VWOs rallying to the call.[41] Our sustained efforts saw a decline of cases involving loansharking and harassment, with a concomitant increase in arrests of loansharks and their runners.[42] The number of loansharking and harassment cases have continued to decline till today.[43]

One of my last acts before I stepped down from office was to send long emails to MinLaw officials setting out what I felt ought to be done to further strengthen our licensing regime to check loansharking behaviour among licensed moneylenders. Hence, I was very happy when, in October 2011 and March 2012, MinLaw implemented some of these suggestions. Still, this will be a continuing battle. Two issues which we had discussed and debated extensively internally were whether to criminalise borrowing from loansharks (at MHA), and whether to lift the cap on interest for small loans made by low-income or no-income borrowers (at MinLaw).[44] Views at that time were divided. On criminalising borrowing, I was not in favour of doing that, although a part of me also acknowledged that it may be difficult to stem the tide if we did not address the issue from both the supply and demand angles (just as we did in the case of drugs). If we did that, prosecution of offenders can then be done judiciously, taking into account the circumstances of the borrower, in particular, why and how much he borrowed. I am glad that with the declining number of harassment cases, this issue has not surfaced since. On lifting the cap on interest for small loans, I was very much against it, on the basis that for these vulnerable people, it was not easy for free market principles to apply. Interestingly, in March 2012, the subsidiary legislation was amended to extend the capping of the allowable interest rate (at an annual rate of 18%) to borrowers earning less than $30,000 a year from $20,000 a year. This indicated MinLaw's thinking, that is, to extend rather than restrict the use of interest rate caps. Then, in October 2015, further changes to the Moneylenders Act limited the maximum interest rate chargeable to four percent a month, regardless of the borrower's income.

At both MHA and MinLaw, I championed the cause of voluntarism. So, other than the "Second Chance man", some called me the "Champion of Volunteers". As President of the Home Team NS Association (HTNSA), I oversaw a period of rapid growth in the HomeTeamNS, both in terms of facilities as well as in membership and activities.[45] Working with a great bunch of "reservists" or operationally-ready NSmen[46] at countless events, we shared many memorable moments and a great sense of camaraderie spanning 18 years. In particular, then Commissioner James Tan, as HTNSA Vice-President, put his heart and soul into the work, for which I remain grateful. At its peak, HTNSA operated six clubhouses spread around Singapore. I also interacted regularly with MHA's volunteers at various functions such as the annual Home Team Connection; National-level CSSP Awards; HomeTeamNS' annual Good Employers Awards, Community Engagement Programme (CEP) training sessions, and countless Civil Defence and Police Volunteer functions. To maintain these warm ties and to raise the involvement of HomeTeam volunteers to the next level, MHA appointed me as Chairman of its HomeTeam Volunteer Network (HTVN) Steering Committee shortly after I retired from politics.[47]

Together with the Singapore Law Society, MinLaw established two Community Legal Clinics (CLCs) in September 2007. Operating from South East Community Development Council (CDC) District and North West CDC District, these clinics operated for four nights a week, manned by volunteer lawyers. By March 2011, about 700 lawyers from 48 firms (including seven Senior Counsel) had volunteered at the two CLCs, rendering legal advice to about 8,700 needy people in all. By 2014, the number of lawyers volunteering had increased to 1,500, committing more than 5,000 man hours to almost 15,000 cases. Plans were announced that year to start at least three more legal clinics, with at least one in each of the five CDCs.[48] Chairing a committee to promote the pro bono spirit in our lawyers, I worked closely with the Law Society towards the goal of having every lawyer contribute at least 25 hours of pro bono work each year. My collaborators on this front were Malathi Das (then Vice-President of the Law Society) and Lim Tanguy (Director of Pro Bono Services in the Law Society). Believing that it was important for lawyers to give back to society, I supported and officiated at the Law Society's annual

Law Awareness Week for many years.[49] It is good to know that so many lawyers and law students are now doing pro bono work.[50]

As in MHA, I agreed to MinLaw's request to continue chairing two Advisory committees overseeing our Community Mediation Centres and the fostering of a pro bono spirit among our lawyers when I stepped down from politics. I have since relinquished the latter appointment. In its stead, I have agreed to be Patron of the RHT Rajan Menon Foundation (the corporate social responsibility arm of law firm, RHT Law Taylor Wessing LLP). This way, I am still involved, in a more direct way, in promoting the pro bono spirit among our lawyers.

Finally, I would like to mention two other policy initiatives where I helped to steer developments and two ground initiatives which have benefited Singaporeans on a daily basis. The two policy initiatives were land acquisition and *en bloc* sales, while the two ground initiatives were opening vacant lands for recreational use and encouraging cycling as a mode of transport.

Land acquisition and *en bloc* sales are two matters very close to Singaporeans' hearts as these concern their properties. For those affected, especially in the case of land acquisition, their lives are turned topsy-turvy. Over the years, there has always been a need for Government to show sensitivity, to assure those affected that it cared about their concerns. I chaired a committee that looked at every case affected by land acquisition to study if it warranted making an *exgratia* payment to soften any financial hardship caused to a landowner which the statutory award could not adequately alleviate. This required patient and careful consideration of every case as no two cases were exactly alike. I spent quite a bit of time doing this, with expert input from officials from the Singapore Land Authority. In particular, I would mention Tay Lee Koon, head of the acquisition team at SLA, who patiently crunched the numbers and made the initial assessment and recommendations.

On *en bloc* sales, Prof Jaya and I moved legislation and responded to many PQs (from as early as 1998)[51] on this equally sensitive topic. We closely monitored sentiments on the ground and suggestions as to how we could further refine our approach. Each time we tweaked our *en bloc* regime, we carefully studied the impact of the amendments on the ground. Indeed, this was one area where getting the balance right was key, that is, on one hand, to maximise our limited land capacity and ensure that our buildings do not become rundown and an eyesore, and on the other, to be economically efficient so that relatively new buildings do not get demolished too readily with its concomitant disruption of settled lifestyles, especially for older residents, and the residents' sense of community living.

Two ground initiatives bring me much satisfaction, even today. At MinLaw, I am happy to have been part of the process that initiated the opening up of vacant lands at our HDB estates and other places for casual and recreational use. This happened when I noticed, while driving around Singapore, that many of these open and vacant lands had a very unfriendly sign "No Trespassing" standing stridently at the edge. While some were indeed not suitable for use, many could in fact be opened up after minor works were carried out on them. I asked the Singapore Land Authority (SLA),[52] which had oversight of these state lands, to do a review. Happily, since 2003, SLA has been opening up state land not required for immediate development for community use. There are now more than 200 such fields listed at www.onemap.sg. The evolution of this policy was accompanied graphically by the sign boards (which had first attracted my attention) being reworded first to "Enter at your own risk" (while better than the earlier sign as it showed flexibility on the Government's part and, quite rightly, putting the onus on the user to take care not to get hurt, it nevertheless still had an unfriendly undertone to it) to "This site is suitable for community and recreational use. Please exercise caution and be responsible for your own safety", (a sensible and reasonable approach). As I drive around Singapore these days, it is a joy for me to see the once empty fields and open spaces filled with happy users flying kites, throwing Frisbees, or kicking footballs around.

Finally, at MHA, together with MP Irene Ng, and with input from agencies such as Police, the Land Transport Authority and the Tampines Town Council, the first seeds were planted in the mid-2000s to create a more bicycle-friendly Singapore. I had taken quite a number of questions on this in Parliament. My recollection was that it was an uphill task at the beginning as everyone was set in his own paradigm. What was required was a mindset adjustment to accommodate the larger use of the ubiquitous bicycle. Not only was there a need to build or reconfigure infrastructure (hardware), more importantly, there was a need to change their mental model, especially when it involved other road users such as pedestrians (sharing of what were essentially pedestrian paths) and motorists (calls to construct dedicated bicycle lanes which would reduce road space). The issue was complicated by the fact that there were different groups of cyclists — from the weekend cyclists comprising families bonding through recreational cycling (often with young children in tow); to older Singaporeans who were cycling around the HDB estates to get to the various amenities; to foreign workers cycling between dormitory/hostel and worksite daily; to Singaporeans cycling from home to MRT station to catch the train to town; to cycling enthusiasts donning special gear on weekends to speed-cycle along long stretches of some of our quieter roads. Our traffic rules adopted a "one size fits all" approach, for example, making it an offence to cycle on a pedestrian pathway, without due regard to who the cyclist was, when it was done, or under what circumstances. There was also insufficient education for motorists and pedestrians on looking out for cyclists. It was tricky but with doggedness and some dexterity, to the credit of all involved, we unpacked the laws, and adopting a practical approach, made the first steps towards promoting greater use of the bicycle. Kudos especially to the then Members of Parliament of Tampines GRC (Mah Bow Tan, Yatiman Yusof, Irene Ng, Ong Kian Min, and Sin Boon Ann), who offered the Division as a test bed for this project which today has gained national significance. Today, it is so good to know that we are moving steadily towards a more bicycle-friendly Singapore.

These days, whenever I meet up with former MHA and MinLaw colleagues, there is so much genuine warmth and nostalgia, recalling past memorable moments together!

Lessons in Leadership

1 I tried to project a facilitative model of leadership. At MinLaw and MHA, I was privileged to have chaired many inter-ministry/inter-agency committees overseeing a wide range of matters. In doing so, I sought to "lead from the front, but sometimes to also come alongside and other times, to just listen and learn from the back", i.e., as a leader, there is a right time to project yourself, a right time to just be part of the pack, and a right time to take a backseat, reflective role. As you lead a diverse team in meetings where the members may not be familiar with one another, as chairman, you set the agenda and guide the flow of discussion. However, you should not dominate or let anyone else dominate the discussion. Rather, you should be a catalyst, putting everyone at ease, so as to facilitate a full and free discussion. At the end of the discussion, you should lead the meeting to come to a consensus as to what has to be done, going forward. This way, over time, as each inter-ministry/inter-agency committee I chaired pressed on with its work, a strong sense of camaraderie and ownership of the issues at hand emerged.

2 There should be mutual respect for fellow leaders. I worked with many civil servants throughout my 18 years in office. Many were bright and motivated, wanting to make Singapore a better place. As political office-holder, I was in the forefront and they were respectful. Still, while they showed respect to the office that I held, I knew that respect for me as a person and leader had to be earned. Any leader must know that at the workplace, colleagues up and down the hierarchy observe and assess you all the time! Do you know your stuff? Are you talking sense? Do you work hard? Are you treating them with decorum and fairness? Do you give them a fair hearing? Are you prepared to listen to contrary views? Are you sufficiently patient and confident to listen to "free-flowing discussion"? You should reflect on how you come across in your dealings with others. What is your persona? Are you seen as an affirming boss? Do you inspire confidence in those who work with you?

3. Put those who work with or under you at ease. Then they will have the impetus to perform, the latitude to be creative, and the motivation to contribute to the common cause. That is the hallmark of a good boss. Do not seek to instil fear in others as a way of gaining respect and getting things done efficiently. That will not get you very far. In addition, embrace ideas from them, as they are stakeholders too! Be receptive to constructive criticisms and "wild" suggestions. Listen carefully and sincerely. Be their friend. Be personable and remember their names. Play and eat with them. Spend informal time of interaction with them! This way, they will not only work for you (which they must do in any case) but also *with* you (which is not always necessarily the case)!

Endnotes

1. In all, I officiated at 18 BOCs between 1999 and 2009.
2. After Deputy Prime Minister (DPM) Teo Chee Hean took over as Minister for Home Affairs in May 2011, after the 2011 GE, he tasked Minister of State (MOS) Masagos Zulkifli to take a fresh look at how we could strengthen our fight against drug abuse, in view of fresh challenges such as the surge in use of synthetic drugs (ice, ecstacy and such) as well as the larger supply of drugs being manufactured in the region, including in clandestine laboratories, and finding their way to Singapore. New measures such as putting soon-to-be-released Long-Term (LT) detainees in Halfway Houses were introduced by the Committee which have enhanced our fight against the drug scourge.
3. All these are documented in *Towards a Drug-Free Singapore: Strategies, Policies and Programs Against Drugs* (NCADA, 1998) and *Slaying the Dragon: Singapore's Fights Against Drugs* (SNP International Publishing Pte. Ltd., 2006).
4. Long-term detention for third-timers and above played its part in the overall scheme by reducing the contamination effect of hardcore addicts on the ground. It was also a strong deterrent message given to second-timers upon their release from DRC that should they relapse one more time, they would face a long prison sentence.
5. The Committee was renamed the Inter-Ministry Committee on Youth Crime (IMYC) in 1998 and the National Committee on Youth Guidance and Rehabilitation (NYGR) in 2008. Then MOS Masagos took over the chairmanship of NYGR when I retired from politics. NYGR's work was taken to the next level when MHA and MYCS formed a Central Youth Guidance Organisation (CYGO) to oversee the countering of youth crime in April 2011.
6. See, for example, *Fighting Youth Crime: A Comparative Study of Two Little Dragons in Asia* (Choi and Lo, 2nd edition, 2004) and *The Right Side: IMC on Youth Crime*, commemorating a decade of Partnership to Rebuild Young Lives (NYC, 2006), and the subsequent edition of *The Right Side 2: 20 years of Rebuilding Lives* (NYC, 2015).
7. Spearheaded by MCYS, Police, AGC and several VWOs, it was introduced in 1997.
8. Spearheaded by Police (CID), AGC and several VWOs, it was introduced in 1997.

9. CRuSH stood for 'Cyberspace Risk and where U Seek Help' and was launched on 11 September 2001, the very day New York's twin towers at the World Trade Centre collapsed. It involved Touch Community Services, the National Youth Council, and MOE to address the emerging troubling phenomenon of internet crime, with youths either as offenders or victim.
10. Much effort was put into ensuring that the road show connected with their intended audience in the schools with valuable input from the National Council of Social Service, National Crime Prevention Council, MOE, and Police. These roadshows were launched in 2006.
11. This was an extensive effort and leveraged on existing mentoring networks in the youth community such as the BP mentoring network and True Hearts Connection, and was launched in 1998.
12. Spearheaded by the Prisons Service, Police and MOE, these visits initiated in 2004 were intended to remind students, especially those who were "at risk" of what awaited them should they end up in prisons.
13. Spearheaded by MOE and SPF, this important scheme was introduced in 1997 to provide school principals with stronger support in tackling delinquency and youth crime problems in their schools.
14. Spearheaded by the then Subordinate Courts and MOE, this programme was introduced in 1996 to promote a culture of mediation and conflict resolution in our secondary schools.
15. *The Right Side 2: 20 years of Rebuilding Lives*, p. 16.
16. This report formed the basic framework upon which then MOS Masagos led another Committee — one that looked at re-offending — that examined the flow of delinquent youths through the system, with some "graduating" from school delinquent behavior to committing minor offences and then on to more serious ones when they grew older.
17. This was over and above the usual one-third remission of the sentence.
18. See Hansard, Parliament No. 10, Session No. 1, Volume No. 78, Sitting No. 3, Title 'Prison (Amendment) Bill 2004' on Sitting Date 9 January 2004 at col 349.
19. It is heartwarming that the momentum we generated has continued. In late 2011, the Law Society of Singapore and the Singapore

My Work at MinLaw and MHA 71

Psychiatric Association initiated a scheme whereby psychiatrists could volunteer their expertise to assess the mental condition of an accused person suspected to be mentally ill. See *The Straits Times*, 16 January 2012, p. B4.
20. This was modelled after the only form of Corrective Work Orders existing then which required litterbugs to pick up litter at public places.
21. See "Inmate numbers fall, thanks to rehabilitation" in *The Straits Times*, 2 February 2011, p. 1.
22. See *The Straits Times*, 13 May 2013, p. A2.
23. See *TODAY*, 19 November 2011, p. 1.
24. See *The Straits Times*, 8 March, 2012 p. C10.
25. *The Straits Times*, 1 April 2015, p. B1. MP Denise Phua was a key proponent of this scheme in Parliament.
26. He must be a first-time offender whose imprisonment does not exceed three months or has been fined not more than $2,000. The offence committed must also not be one listed under the Third Schedule of the Registration of Criminals Act.
27. The key AGC officer involved was Owi Beng Ki, who was steady and reliable.
28. Under the Nurses Registration Act.
29. Published by ICC Publishing SA and Oceania Publications Inc.
30. They originally operated from three premises at the URA Centre (CMC Central), Woodlands Civic Centre (Regional North) and the Subordinate Courts. Now, they are centralised in one centre at URA, which is easily accessible.
31. A record 545 students from almost 70 schools participated in the fifth forum in the series in September 2010.
32. Under this scheme, more than 60 companies have pledged to consider using mediation to resolve their disputes.
33. The industries covered include healthcare, private education, estate agents and sports.
34. For representatives from institutions, it was intended that they would be rotated amongst the key institutions. The Insurance Disputes Resolution Organisation (IDRO) and the Singapore Institute of Building were the first such institutional members appointed.
35. The premises were opened for business in August 2007 and was conceived collaboratively by Professor Jayakumar and then Chief Justice Chan Sek Keong. Then Permanent Secretary Chan Lai Fung

also pushed for it with her colleagues in the Ministry of Finance. I played a supportive role.

36. *The Straits Times*, 7 October, C9, 2 January 2011.
37. *The Straits Times*, 26 February 2015.
38. The number of harassment cases surged from 9,400 in 2007 to 11,400 in 2008, and reached an all-time high of 17,900 in 2009. Thereafter, it stabilised and came down to about 15,500 in 2010. Our relentless efforts paid off as the number dipped 24% to 11,800 in 2011. In 2014, the number had dipped further to 5,763.
39. For a loan of $1,000, if the interest was 20%, the amount the borrower actually received was only $800.
40. In November 2008 and January 2010.
41. The grassroots momentum created has continued. For example, *TODAY* reported on 4 March 2012 at page 14 that with more volunteers going on patrol under the Citizens On Patrol programme, the complaints of loansharking activities had dropped in Bukit Panjang constituency.
42. The number of loansharking and harassment cases dipped 21% from 16,834 in 2010 to 13,342 in 2011. On the other hand, the number of arrests rose by 31% from 1,508 to 1,981 persons over the same period. (See Police Annual Crime brief, as reported, for example in *The Straits Time*, 8 February 2011, p. A8.)
43. In 2015, UML-related harassment cases registered a 10-year low, with 4,229 cases down 26% from 5,763 cases in 2014.
44. When we lifted the cap on interest generally in 2008, we retained the cap of 18% interest for loans up to $3,000 taken out by those who earned less than $20,000 a year or had no income.
45. When I became President of the Singapore Police Reservists' Association (SPRA) and Civil Defence Reservists' Association (CDRA) in 1993, we were in rented premises at Marina Bayfront and the Paragon. In 2005, SPRA and CDRA (by then renamed SPANS and CDANS) merged to form the Home Team NS Association (HTNSA). By May 2011, HTNSA operated from six premises spread across Singapore, that is, two full-facilities clubhouses at Bukit Batok and Balestier, a complex of chalets at Pasir Ris and three satellite clubhouses at Sembawang, UE Square and Chinatown. Our membership stood at a high of 180,000 in May 2011. We now have a 9-hole course named after us at a new Kranji golf course that was built in 2005. On this, I am grateful to SAFRA for its magnanimity in

changing the name of the former SAFRA golf club at Tanah Merah to the National Service Resort Country Club. This magnanimous gesture signals to all our NSmen, whether in the Police or SAF, that they work alongside each other in keeping Singapore safe and secure, both internally and from external threats.

46. Personally, I much prefer the term "reservists" which everyone readily understood. The new nomenclature is a mouthful and does not resonate at all!
47. SGSecure, a national movement to involve every Singaporean to keep Singapore safe and secure was launched in September 2016. A year or so before that, I had positioned HTVN to do that and exhorted all HTVN members to be change agents for that cause.
48. See *The Straits Times*, 13 September 2014, p. B14.
49. Early on in 1994, my first "blockhead" (which is something like a monitor) at Block C, Kent Ridge Hall (where I was a Resident Fellow from 1981 to 1987), "Cheenu" called on me at MinLaw, requesting my help to support their first Law Awareness event. He was chairman of the Law Awareness event that year. I gladly did what I could to help.
50. See *The Straits Times*, 12 January 2016, p. B4.
51. See my parliamentary reply to Lew Syn Pau on 19 February 1998.
52. Current High Court Registrar Vincent Hoong was the Chief Executive of SLA then who carried the ball and ran with it.

Chapter 4 | # DEBATING IN PARLIAMENT

Sir, we should be mindful that Singaporeans respond to the Next Lap differently. Some, like me, find the vision inspiring, others find it bewildering. Some look forward eagerly to the Next Lap. Others are wary. They fear that they cannot adjust. I hope that this will be borne in mind as specific programmes are further firmed up and shared with the public. As we level upwards, we should be mindful that Singaporeans have different levels of capacity to enjoy the good life. Also, in our pursuit of market oriented pragmatic policies, we should be prepared to exercise flexibility and compassion in enforcing the rules against genuine hardship cases, for indeed genuine hardship cases there will always be. On these premises, Sir, I firmly believe that there is a place under the sun in Singapore for everyone.

An excerpt from my maiden speech in Parliament in January 1992

Just as we have a ministry to look after the arts, Government should seriously consider tasking, if not setting up separately, a ministry to look after sports. Sports — like the arts — permeates national life and is not a sectoral concern... Achieving sports excellence is a complex matter requiring total commitment. Focusing priorities, setting targets, channelling limited resources, nurturing champions, lining up sponsors and keeping them happy, coordinating the NSAs, arbitrating disputes, guiding Singapore sports into the era of professionalism — and of course, continuing the important task of ensuring healthy lifestyles for all Singaporeans — these require the attention of more than a minister in charge of a large ministry (MCD), hardworking though he is, who is also concurrently the Minister for Health... sportsmen, like performing artistes, have a certain emotional mould that requires sensitive handling... Even if Government considers the setting up of another ministry not necessary, I would suggest that perhaps they should put forward a minister who can be the Sports Supremo in Singapore, much as Minister George Yeo and Professor Tommy Koh are heroes in the arts scene....

My speech in Parliament as a backbencher in March 1993
that was selected as the "Speech of the Day", *The Straits Times*, 19 March 1993

I enjoyed your presentation — pointed, convincing and expressive. Your command of tone and text was impressive...

NMP Claire Chiang with whom I had interesting debates in Parliament

Debating in Parliament

As an office-holder, I was very busy in Parliament too.

At both Ministries, a key responsibility assigned to me was to respond to parliamentary questions (PQs). I took most of the PQs at both Ministries. Many were filed, especially at MHA. Being an operational Ministry overseeing the overall safety and security of Singapore, its coverage was considerably wider than most of the other Ministries. Moreover, many things that happened in Singapore under MHA's purview impacted Singaporeans. Hence, many MPs — fellow PAP MPs, opposition MPs, Nominated MPs as well as Non-Constituency MPs — filed questions for reply by MHA. The scope of the PQs I took were wide-ranging. They included traffic congestion at the land checkpoints, alleged police brutality against accused persons, violence against women, impounding of passports, use of the Speakers' Corner, state of driving in Singapore, youth crime and juvenile delinquency, long-term passes and permanent residence rejections, death penalty, drug abuse and crime statistics, prison population, the illegal moneylending or loansharking situation, prostitution, measures to counter ill-effects of casinos, and human trafficking.

In all, I responded to some 190 PQs (filed at MHA and MinLaw) throughout my 18 years as office-holder. If I am not wrong, this could be one of the highest, if not the highest, number taken by an office-holder, including Cabinet Ministers, during that period. This works out roughly to about one PQ for every parliamentary session I attended! Parliament generally sat once a month. The few days before the sitting would find me rather edgy and tense. I would then joke with my wife that I was having "menstrual pain"! Still, even though I would be very busy the few days before each monthly parliamentary sitting, finalising the replies and preparing responses to possible supplementary questions (the MP who had filed the PQ or, indeed, any other MP could follow up with further queries after I had read out my prepared reply), it was a great learning experience each time I did it. It meant that I mastered the subject matter because of this constant exposure in the House, standing on my feet to explain and defend my replies. I am thankful for friends like NMP Claire Chiang who, early on in my political career, encouraged me with a short note as follows "I enjoyed your presentation — pointed, convincing and expressive. Your command of tone and text was impressive..."

A difficult speech that I had to make in Parliament was my response during the Committee of Supply debate in 2001 to a "cut" that Mr Shanmugam, then MP for Sembawang GRC, had made to the MinLaw budget.[1] He had argued that instead of mandatory imprisonment for harbourers of illegal immigrants and over-stayers, our laws should be amended to give our Courts discretion whether they should be sent to jail. In 2001, our anti-harbouring laws were very strict as the situation was dire. As I explained in my reply to Mr Shanmugam, I urged him and others like him who argued for a more lenient approach to look at "the big picture". The nature and magnitude of our illegal immigrant offender problem at that time justified a tough approach. In 2000, we had arrested 16,500 illegal immigrant offenders (as a comparison, in 2010, the number of arrests had dropped to less than 3,000). Thus, even though we knew that there were Singaporeans who felt discomfort that our strict laws had caused some ordinary Singaporeans who may not have possessed a criminal intent to go to jail,[2] government felt that lifting the mandatory imprisonment requirement would send the wrong signal, and would put Singapore and Singaporeans at risk. It was a difficult speech for me to make because, deep inside, I too felt some discomfort that our anti-harbouring laws were too strict. Moreover, as Mr Shanmugam did not speak very much in Parliament,[3] the media tended to cover him extensively when he did. Also, it was a topic very much in the news, and as he puts it: "This legislation, which seeks to send a variety of people to jail without seeking to distinguish those who are negligent and those who are morally culpable, has caused many right-thinking people to be concerned..."[4] I knew that there was a groundswell of public support for a more lenient, flexible approach.[5] I was therefore concerned how the media would report on our debate the following day. That day (9 March 2001), we had a good debate. His was a hard-hitting but fairly-put speech. My response was, I should think, as robust and fairly-put as well. In any case, the media the following day, as I had expected, gave prominent coverage to our debate. That both of us made valid points contributed to a balanced report. This debate stands out because, a few years after it took place, Government decided to soften the punishment regime for harbouring immigration offenders by removing the mandatory imprisonment if the act of harbouring was carried out "negligently". A key reason was that the numbers had come down so that the need for a strong deterrent punishment was less pressing. Moreover, with greater publicity focused on the problem and the attendant negative consequences, the need for tough, inflexible punishment had become less necessary. This is a good example of a tough punishment, necessary when introduced, being moderated over time. As Government has said many times, our laws our not cast in stone!

Throughout my 18 years as office-holder, I participated fully every year in the Committee of Supply debate, helping to defend and explain MinLaw and MHA policies. As both Prof Jaya and Mr Wong were senior members of the Cabinet, debate on the two Ministries' budget and policies always came early (this is because, during my time, the Ministries were set down in the Order Paper according to the seniority of the Minister in charge), thus leaving me with less time to prepare. It also came one after the other (as they were pegged one after the other in seniority), and that left me with little time to recover in between the two Ministries' debates. Those one to two days of rigorous debate found me really exhausted! Still, I thoroughly enjoyed them, as well as the prior weeks of preparation, as they helped me to understand MinLaw and MHA policies and actions much better! The crux of the matter is really that it is right that backbenchers hold office-holders to account, filing "cuts" to get them to explain and defend the policies that they formulate and implement. Thus, even though PAP MPs may dominate Parliament in terms of numbers, the element of accountability on the part of Government has always been there, even more so nowadays, with a more discerning electorate wishing to see their elected representatives being more active in Parliament.

At MinLaw, even though I took fewer PQs, some of the matters that I addressed, such as land acquisition and *en bloc* sales, were potentially sensitive ones and had to be carefully handled. Other MinLaw PQs included discharge from bankruptcy, use of state land and premises, and extending legal aid to more Singaporeans. The latter came under the rubric of "access to justice", which was a recurrent topic in Parliament, pressed by MPs from all backgrounds — government, opposition, and nominated.

There were other memorable moments in the House. I remember an early occasion in 1994 during the Committee of Supply debate in March when I responded to a follow-up question by Dr Kanwaljit Soin, then Nominated Member of Parliament (fondly called "Karny" by those of us who knew her well) on the issue of spousal violence, that is, women who were physically abused in their homes by their husbands. The way my response came out as reported in the media was that there was no need for Police to respond immediately to every "999" call for help from a physically abused wife. This raised the spectre of a hapless wife calling Police on the telephone, pleading to Police to intervene quickly to shield her from the blows of an enraged husband who was assaulting her, only for Police to respond with a *laissez faire* "wait and see" attitude! Of course, this was not what I meant. The situation I intended to describe was one where the assault had already taken place sometime earlier, and the wife was making a report at the police station. When this happened, there was no need for Police to accompany the wife straightaway to her home to investigate the matter. What needed to be done then was to advise the aggrieved wife to lodge a magistrates' complaint.

My response, as portrayed, expectedly drew ire and criticism from readers in the press, painting me in a negative light, as one who was uncaring and unsympathetic. I felt alarmed and wronged, and regretted that I had not explained my position more clearly. A subsequent letter issued by MHA clarified my reply and assured the public that the Police took a serious view of spousal violence. The lesson here is that what we say in Parliament, and how we say it can leave lingering impressions in the public's mind, shaping public opinion of our persona as office-holders. Though painful at that time, there was a silver lining to this episode. After this debate took place, MHA initiated an inter-Ministry working group that saw Police work closely with women's groups such as the Singapore Council of Women's Organisations (SCWO) and the Association of Women for Action and Research (AWARE) to improve and streamline procedures on the ground so that abused spouses could seek help more easily.

A speech that made it as "Speech of the Day" in *The Straits Times* was one that I made as a backbencher in 1993 (see brief excerpts in the opening of this chapter). That made my day as I had spoken from the heart and had suggested what appeared then to be against the tide of Government thinking! I share more of this in Chapter 5.

I must add that sometimes I caused Mr Wong some anxiety. This was because I would enter the Chamber just before my PQ, as set down on the Order Paper, was to be answered! Driving down to Parliament Lane from the New Phoenix Park at Thomson, I would try to time my arrival in Parliament a few minutes before responding to the PQ. This enabled me to do more work in my office. Mr Wong would be glancing over his shoulders to see if I was at my seat. Thankfully, notwithstanding some anxious moments, I never let him down by missing any PQ. Such is the steady working relationship between us that this never became a point of conflict. I would like to think that this was because both he (and Prof Jaya) knew that they could rely on me, as a colleague, to do my job well in the House.[6]

Other than replying to PQs, I was also kept busy taking Bills through Parliament. In all, I took about 75 Bills through Parliament. Here, again, if I am not wrong, this could be one of the highest, if not the highest, taken by any office-holder during that period. It averaged out to about one Bill every two to three parliamentary sessions (excluding the annual Budget and

Committee of Supply debates that spanned two weeks or so when Bills were seldom read a second/third time).[7] The Bills that I took at both Ministries spanned a wide range of subjects, including criminal procedure, sale of goods, arbitration, coroners' inquiries, legal profession, miscellaneous amendments to non-MinLaw statutes, small claims tribunals, bankruptcy, moneylending, land surveyors, *en bloc* sales procedures, official secrets, evidence and procedures, land titles, and processes in the Subordinate and Supreme Courts.

The major Bills with greater impact that I took through were:
(1) The Penal Code amendments in 2007. This was the largest law reform project I had oversight of; it stretched over three to four years, involving the review of all 500 provisions of the Penal Code as well as other related statues, where we engaged in extensive public consultation. The debate in the House stretched over two days when 21 MPs, including the PM, spoke. A non-amendment, Section 377A, concerning sex between men became one of the hottest issues in the debate;
(2) Five-yearly extensions of the Criminal Law (Temporary Provisions) Act. The Act has a "sunset clause" whereby the Bill expires every five years unless extended for another five years after the House is satisfied that there is a continued need for it. I took it through three times over my 18 years in MHA, the last renewal being on January 2009;
(3) Several extensive amendments to the Moneylenders Act. I oversaw this Act at both MHA and MinLaw. At MinLaw, the amendments sought to modernise the moneylending regime, while at MHA, the focus was on stamping out loansharking/ illegal moneylending. Actually, it was incongruous that the same piece of legislation addressed two diverse situations with their different attendant problems. However, this underscored the complementarity of MinLaw and MHA and how some of their matters overlapped, often in strategic ways. This made my work that much more interesting! It is rare that an office-holder in two Ministries moves extensive amendments in the same piece of legislation in his different capacities;

(4) About 12 Bills on various aspects of intellectual property (IP) such as formation of the Intellectual Property Academy (IPA), revamp of our Copyrights, Trademarks and Patent law, introduction of IP rights over geographical indications, layout designs of integrated circuits and registered design. These were Bills that we had to pass so that Singapore could comply with the standards required under the Agreement on Trade-related Aspects of Intellectual Property (TRIPS) within the time frame set (1995–1999). Each time I took a Bill, I had to bone up on the IP law in question as the issues were very technical in nature;[8]

(5) The Coroners Act. We re-scoped the Coroner's jurisdiction and changed the nature of the inquiry from a fault-finding to a fact-finding one. This was a fundamental change;

(6) Community Mediation Act. I had chaired a Committee which recommended the setting up of community mediation centres to mediate relational disputes on the ground, such as those between neighbours. This was an early key piece in an unfolding collage, which has now emerged as a comprehensive approach to handling relational disputes in a compact, fast-paced multi-racial, multi-religious Singapore. The Community Disputes Resolution Tribunals, which commenced on 1 October 2015, is the latest piece in this collage.

(7) Successive amendments to the Bankruptcy Act, to strike a better and fairer balance between the legitimate interests of a bankrupt (especially one arising from business failure) and those of the creditors and society as a whole;

(8) Amendments to the Legal Aid and Assistance Act (to loosen the criteria for qualification for legal aid) so that more people would qualify for legal aid; and

(9) Amendments to refine and improve our arbitration regimes, both domestic and international.

I was thrust into debating and defending MHA and MinLaw Bills in a memorable way. This came early in February 1996 when, as a newly-promoted Senior Parliamentary Secretary, I took the

Miscellaneous Offences (Public Order and Nuisance) (Amendment) Bill. One of the provisions in the Bill created a new offence of appearing nude in public or exposed to the public view. Nominated Member of Parliament (NMP) Walter Woon had earlier indicated to Parliament that he would be speaking at Committee stage to amend the Bill's provisions. Being a provision that criminalised behaviour, even inadvertent behaviour, he felt it should be more tightly worded.[9] As that was one of the earlier Bills I was taking, I did not realise that what Professor Woon proposed to do was rather unusual, that is, speaking at Committee stage to amend the Bill on a substantive point. As such, I should have been fully prepared to respond to Walter's arguments in the House. As I knew Walter well from our time as colleagues at the Law Faculty, I could have spoken to him to get more details from him as to what he intended to say. Being the gentleman that he is, he would have shared his thoughts with me. However, I did not. Hence, in retrospect, I think my response to his arguments was not as convincing as they could and should have been. His amendment was, however, not carried and the provision remains a wide one. However, as far as I can recall, this provision has not been invoked in the context that Walter had envisaged.

In my parliamentary work, I am grateful for an easy and generally relaxed relationship with the many people I interacted with, both in the chambers of the House and outside of it. Whether it was Clerk of Parliament PO Ram and his successor, Ng Sheau Jiuan (and their staff), the librarians Mrs Chia-Khoo Sait Poh and Mrs Yang Soh Bee who were extremely helpful, the attendants such as Guna and Yian Lan, the different batches of MPs through the years — whether Government, Opposition or nominated (some of whom such as Lim Biow Chuan, Sylvia Lim, and Simon Tay were my former students) — as well as key officers in MHA and MinLaw who "staffed" my parliamentary work, overall, I really enjoyed my interactions with them. This in turn made for better debates, both in terms of the process as well as the outcomes — whether it was doing last-minute research in the

Parliament library, calling an MHA or MinLaw officer during the break for a point that I was not sure about, reviewing and getting further input for my supplementary responses while preparing for the debates, or the actual process of taking a Bill through Parliament, responding to a PQ, or to the many "cuts" filed during Committee of Supply debate.

Another highlight of my time in the House was taking seven substantive Motions that were filed by Mr Jeyaretnam when he returned to Parliament after the 1996 General Election as a Non-Constituency MP. Mr Jeyaretnam had vacated his seat in 1986 when he was convicted of an offence. He made up for lost time by filing a host of PQs and Motions when he returned, and I responded to most of them! This was because the main focus of his Motions was on the Judiciary and our laws. They included "Respect for the Judiciary", "Setting Up of a Commission of Inquiry into Methods of Investigation and the Law to Ascertain if There Were Adequate Safeguards for Accused Persons Who May Be Innocent", "Removal of Fear in People's Lives" and "Commission to Examine our Defamation Laws". I think it irked him that, unlike the previous time when he was in the House and had occasion to debate and cross swords with Mr Lee Kuan Yew (who was then PM) and Prof Jaya, a Cabinet Minister, this time round, he had to contend with, in his own words, "a junior Minister". Unlike Adjournment Motions where the total speaking time is capped at 30 minutes, for Main Motions, speakers can speak for extended periods, to present one's case and rebut other MPs' points. I recall one occasion when we ended our debate at 9.30 pm! That was when we were still in the Old Parliament House, where fiery and lengthy debates had raged in the early days of Singapore's self-governance and independence. On that occasion, I remember I felt somewhat nostalgic that I had the opportunity to experience a little of what our pioneer MPs and Ministers had gone through, albeit at a less intense level for sure! I put a lot of effort into preparing for these debates as I had to envisage what Mr Jeyaretnam would say and, in my replies, not say anything sensational or so newsworthy as to grab the headlines. On this, I think I succeeded!

Over a period of seven years, from 1998 to 2005, Parliament responded to several queries from the Inter-Parliamentary Union's (IPU) Committee on Human Rights on Mr Jeyaretnam's situation in Singapore. IPU has a process whereby any Parliamentarian who feels he has been unfairly treated in his home country can initiate action to have his case heard before the Committee. At the IPU's bi-annual conferences, MPs attending from countries against which complaints have been lodged may be required to appear before the Committee to respond orally to any further queries it may have on a case it was looking at. The Committee was made up of MPs from different countries whose Parliaments were members of the IPU. I provided input to Parliament as it drafted the responses to these queries and also briefed our MPs who were attending these meetings.

Indeed, Mr Jeyaretnam and I were quite inseparable. When he was invited to speak (as a member of an Opposition party in Singapore) in Manila at an "International Conference of Asian Political Parties" in the year 2000, I was there as a member of the ruling party to respond to his points. Imagine the surprise on his face when I slipped quietly into the seat next to him and said "Hello, Mr Jeyaretnam!" Notwithstanding our frequent "skirmishes", I must say that, on the whole, we were both gentlemanly. Unlike the early years in Parliament when Mr Jeyaretnam clashed with the "big guns", there was little acrimony, bitterness, or sarcasm shown between us. For this, I am thankful.

Sometimes, I do miss the cut and thrust of Parliamentary debate.

Lessons in Leadership

1. We must be competent in whatever we do at work. That is an important starting point. Having mastery of our work knowledge domain is very important. Then we will gain the respect and confidence of our fellow workers, including our bosses and subordinates. We should also always prepare well for any assignment, whether it is a presentation, meeting or interview. There are no shortcuts. Being able to articulate and, if necessary, debate and defend a point of view is something all of us should cultivate. We need not be a great debater, or smooth talker. Making good sense in an assured, steady tone is a good start. We should not be personal even as we seek to win the argument. If we make friends of our adversaries, even if grudging ones, so much the better! Be prepared, not only in terms of mastering the materials, but also mentally.

2. When we speak, whether in formal settings or otherwise, we should speak from the heart. When we do this, our sincerity and earnestness will come through. Even when we read from a script, we should do so in an easy, relaxed manner so that it sounds less like rote reading. Go at a good pace, not too rushed. *Ad lib* to expand on your points, where appropriate; look up often to connect with the audience.

3. All aspiring leaders should read widely. Read beyond your professional interests. Hone your intellectual quotient (IQ). Still, it is when your IQ, EQ (emotional quotient) and SQ (social quotient) are in fine balance, that you can function at an optimum as a leader. When you read, once in a while, mouth the words! Yes, *literally* read. Once in a while, it is good to hear yourself and assess how you sound. Sometimes, you are pleasantly surprised. Most times, you will know that you need to improve so as to sound better. Be brutally honest and you will become a better and more effective speaker.

Endnotes

1. Each year, the Committee of Supply (COS) debate follows on after the Budget Debate which normally takes two to three days. The COS debate takes about 10 days. During this period, MPs will raise "cuts" (make short speeches of one- to five-minutes duration) questioning a Ministry's policies, often making useful suggestions on fine-tuning them. For the larger Ministries like MOE and MHA, MPs were likely to make 25 to 30 cuts each year. For a small Ministry like MinLaw, the average number of cuts each year was about 10 to 15. As there were only Prof Jaya and me in MinLaw, and only three officeholders in MHA (other than Mr Wong and myself, in most years at various times, there was a third officeholder, for example, Mr Mohamad Maidin (Senior Parliamentary Secretary), Mr Harun Ghani (Politiical Secretary), Mr Shanmugam (Second Minister) and Mr Masagos Zulkifli (Minister of State), I was very busy during this time.
2. They included a church worker who was a deacon (the first case to really cause a public outcry), professionals such as an accountant and even an elderly lady who was in her 70s.
3. Due to his busy work as a top legal practitioner.
4. Hansard, Vol. 73, Col. 523.
5. This was especially the case after much public sympathy had surfaced following the imprisonment term imposed on a "full-time" church deacon, Seow Boon Wah, in 1999.
6. There was no such problem with my MinLaw PQs, as I would very often be at my MinLaw office at the Treasury Building on Hill Street before heading to Parliament House just across the road.
7. A Bill is introduced at its first reading. It is placed before the House for MPs' scrutiny. At the next sitting of Parliament which is normally a month or so later, it is debated, taken through by the office-holder and normally passed by the House at successive second and third readings. This would be the case unless the Bill was sent to Select Committee, which normally did not happen.
8. There was a spate of Intellectual Property Bills to take through Parliament because we were working within a fairly tight timeline (1995 and 1999) to amend our laws to render them TRIPS-compliant. "TRIPS" stands for the Agreement on Trade-Related Aspects of Intellectual Property Rights. It is an international agreement administered by the World Trade Organisation (WTO) that sets down

minimum standards for many forms of intellectual property (IP) regulations such as protection, remedies and enforcement.
9. For example, a person who is still naked after bathing and, standing near his window or balcony, is seen drying himself by his neighbour could possibly be prosecuted under the provisions of the new Act.

Hurdling in National Junior College (NJC); second from right.

Performing in "Barretts of Wimpole Street" during the NJC Drama Festival in 1971. Jane Ittogi (now married to DPM Tharman Shanmugaratnam) is seated on the sofa.

Mingling with residents at the Nee Soon East courtyard.

Getting up close with the children of Nee Soon East.

Exchanging greetings with coffee shop patrons at Nee Soon East.

Introducing Mr Patrick Tay, who is taller, more handsome and sings better, to residents of Nee Soon East.

With Mr Wong Kan Seng and the two VPs of the Home Team NS Association, Commissioners Khoo Boon Hui and James Tan — visioning for HTNSA?

With Prof Jaya and Commissioner James Tan in the early days of the Civil Defence Reservist Association.

Opening an event with a mighty football kick!

Hamming it up with the event contestants of the Strongman Challenge.

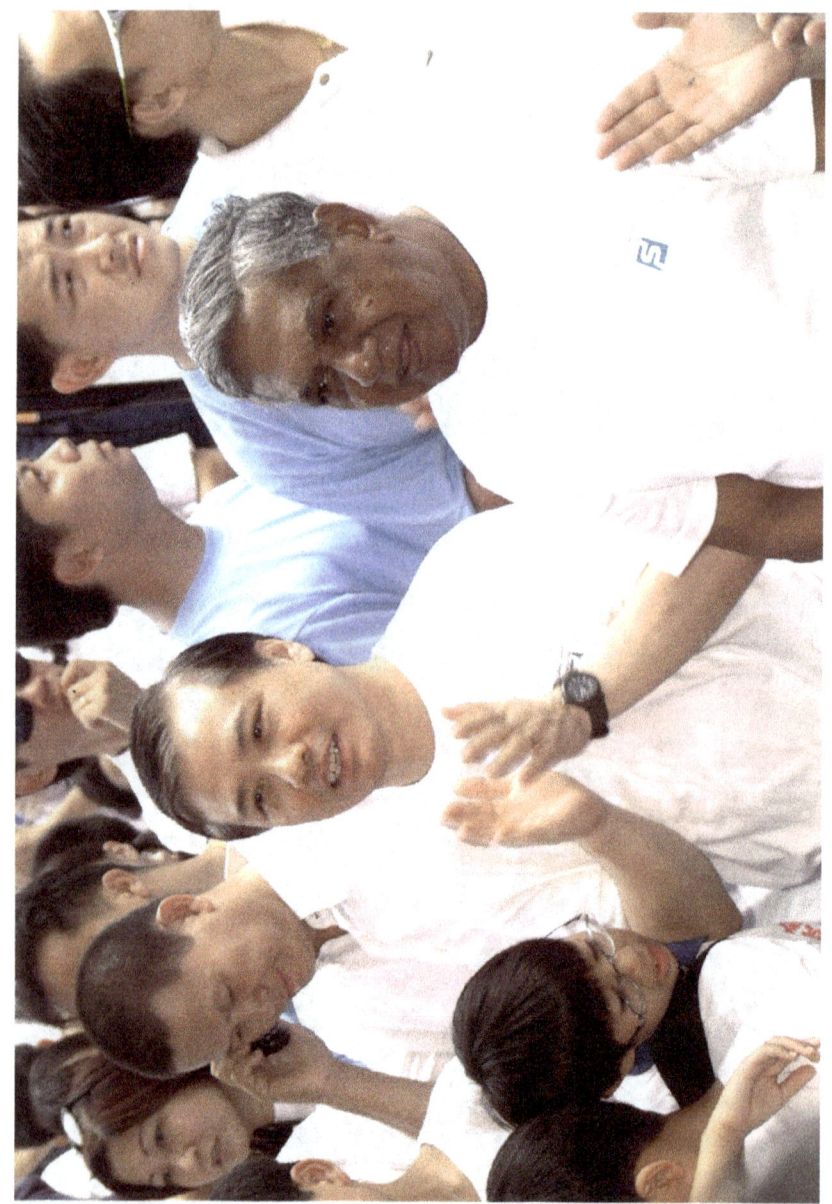

With the late Mr SR Nathan, who was a strong supporter of the Home Team NS Association.

A recent photo with the Home Team Volunteer Network (HTVN) volunteers.

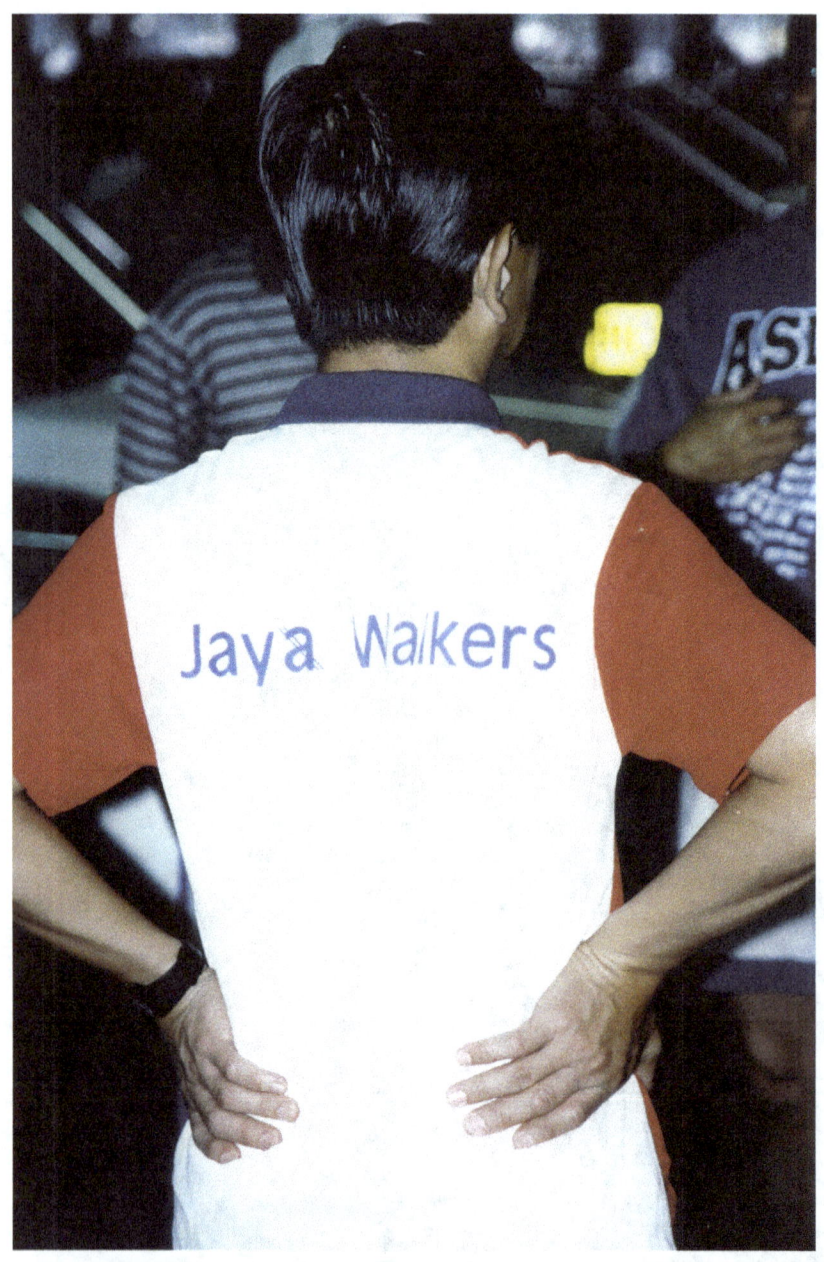

The t-shirt worn by the Jaya Walkers — the *gelek* kings — at The New Paper Big Walk (seen here as worn by Mr Wong Kan Seng). Source: *The New Paper* © Singapore Press Holdings Limited. Permission required for reproduction.

The Singapore LIONS circa 2007.

Sharing with youths as FAS President during a session at Ba'alwie Mosque, hosted by Ustaz Habib Hassan.

Performing a song with Hall Fellows and friends at a concert.

Hosting students carolling in the Master's flat during Christmas…with the little ones joining in too!

Chatting informally with students at a games court with my daughter in tow.

Bidding farewell to Nee Soon East upon retiring from politics.

Chapter 5 | IMPACTING SINGAPOREANS IN OTHER WAYS

I am very encouraged by the passion and the huge amount of energy out there, waiting to be harnessed into a positive force for the good of sports in Singapore... we're climbing a mountain and are one-fifth up. It gets tougher as we go up, but the view also gets more exhilarating and exciting. Let's climb this mountain together. Different members will look at different sides, different views and perspectives, but all going only one way — forward and always upwards.

Opening a seminar that presented recommendations of the Committee on Sporting Singapore Report, 24 February 2001

The second programme aims to assist families of offenders. When an offender is in prison or DRC, his family may have no one to turn to for support. And when the offender is a key member of the family, a host of other social problems may result. For example, his children, for lack of guidance, can mix with bad company or turn to crime. Under this Community & Support Program for Offenders' Families (CFP) initiative, CDC volunteers will help the family by providing emotional support, counselling, childcare and financial assistance. The early involvement of CDC volunteers can help prevent the breakdown of an offender's family.

Launching a programme which evolved into the Community Outreach Project, 31 July 1998

The large majority of Singaporean employers do not mistreat their foreign domestic workers (FDW). A small minority may... Some may not realise their actions' impact on the overall well-being of their FDW. Some may think there is nothing wrong with their actions. There is a need for greater understanding and sensitivity on their part. Even for the many Singaporean employers who do not mistreat their FDWs, with greater understanding and thoughtful reflection, the relationship can be an even better one... To help Singaporean employers come to grips with this social phenomenon, Sembawang-Hong Kah CDC has pieced together a series of events to help enhance the working relationship between employers and their FDWs.

Launching the two-month "Maid-A-Friend" programme to enhance the relationship between employers and their FDWs, 5 May 2001

I agreed to be their Patron because here was a group of leaders from NUS' Halls of Residence who had channelled their youthful idealism into a worthy cause. Despite just having graduated from the University and finding their feet in working life, they remained committed to their vision. I have seen the group (Children's Cancer Foundation) grow from strength to strength, sincere in its desire to lend a helping hand... More young people should do likewise. Channel youthful idealism and energy into worthwhile projects that touch lives. The transition from studies to work should not spell the death of community service, sports or arts in one's life...When Singaporeans help each other through community service, we affirm each other and send a powerful personal message — "I care for you. Your happiness matters to me..."

Children's Cancer Foundation's Millennium Fundraising Event, 31 December 1999

Impacting Singaporeans in Other Ways

Other than discharging my duties and responsibilities at MHA and MinLaw, and tending to the ground at Nee Soon East, I had the privilege of wearing several hats that impacted Singapore and Singaporeans' lives in other ways. As in the earlier phases of my life, I stretched myself fully, thankful for the opportunities that came my way. As was my experience in ACS, NJC and the Singapore University, I did not just focus on my core responsibilities ("studying" in my school days and discharging my responsibilities at MHA, MinLaw and the PAP in politics), but lived life fully by immersing myself in activities in line with my passion, which fit my temperament, and where I felt could make Singapore a better place.[1] As a student, I was active in sports, student leadership, drama and debates. My active involvement in these pursuits received some recognition when I was selected as a finalist in the Outstanding Young Singaporean Award organised by the Singapore Jaycees in 1974. I was then a national service officer, competing against much more accomplished older nominees with a more established track record.[2] Other than my Ministry work and constituency work at Nee Soon East, I pursued other worthwhile causes. I would have lived a less satisfying life and would have left a weaker political legacy if not for these areas of involvement.

My key areas of involvement in civic organisations included stints as Deputy Chairman of the Committee on Sporting Singapore (2000 to 2002), President of the Football Association of Singapore (2004 to 2009), Board member of the National Youth Achievement Award or NYAA (1996 to 2012), Patron of the Children's Cancer Foundation (1996 till now), Ling Kwang Home for Senior Citizens, Singapore Christian Home and Bishan Home for the Intellectually Disabled, Advisor of Ho See Seng Tong Clan Association (where my father was a leader when he was alive in the 1960s and early 1970s) and Chairman of the Kreta Ayer People's Theatre Foundation Management Committee since 1996 (I stepped down as MC chairman in January 2012 but continue to sit on the Board of Governors till today). I had launched Heartware Network in 2000, a youth organisation that promoted youth voluntarism, enterprise and development and supported many of their events as Guest-of-Honour. In addition to these social sector hats, I chaired the Sembawang–Hong Kah Community Development Council (CDC) from 1997 to 2001, the People's Action Party Community Foundation (PCF) Executive Committee from 1996 to 2007 and Sembawang Town Council (1997–1999; 2001–2003).[3] In the PAP, I was Second Organising Secretary from 2001 to 2008 (working closely with the Executive Director, Lau Ping Sum) and a member of the Party's Central Executive Committee from 2004 to 2008. During those days, I literally lived each day at a time, with a packed schedule that required me to keep changing my "hats".

I tried to add value in all these appointments — guiding, facilitating, connecting, and giving perspectives. Let me focus on what I consider my key contributions in these areas of "Extra-Curricular Activities (ECA)". One area of involvement I am particularly proud of is my chairmanship of the Sembawang–Hong Kah CDC. As in the case of other groups of volunteers, those who stepped up to the plate to volunteer their expertise and time to uplift the lives of a fifth of Singapore's total population living in the CDC were an exemplary lot. Indeed, we were a big CDC — in fact, the biggest — occupying almost a fourth of Singapore's land area, comprising two large GRCs and several single wards. Well supported by a committed core of CDC staff headed by Sng Chan Kiah, we launched many innovative programs and activities that touched lives in a real way. I will just mention four groundbreaking ones.

The first was the formation of brisk walking groups. Quite early on as CDC chairman, I had conceived the idea of forming brisk walking groups to achieve three key purposes. First, as a form of exercise that everyone from the young to the old could do; second, I saw it as good way to promote good neighbourliness, as neighbours in the same residents' zone came together, gathering at the Residents' Committee (RC) centre every morning or at least twice a week or so, to walk around the neighbourhood; and third, it was a useful and very meaningful way to welcome new neighbours and to get to know them.[4] As I explained to the CDC Council when I first raised this idea, this should be left as decentralised and as informal as possible. Hence, RCs should take the lead. To make the walk more interesting, they should recce and sketch out three routes starting from the RC. Each should be of a different length and take the walkers to different parts of the neighbourhood. Every time the walkers get together, they can decide which route to take. This way, we launched the first brisk walking clubs in Singapore in the late 1990s, officiated by then DPM Tony Tan, who was the Minister-in-Charge of Sembawang GRC and the neighbouring SMCs in the north. At our launch, we featured a national female walker, Madhavy Nair, a Police Officer and grassroots leader who, together with another keen walker in his 70s, "strutted their stuff" on stage, much to the crowd's delight! To enthuse residents to take up brisk walking, we had these groups all come together once in a while, so that as they saw the growing numbers of faithful walkers of all ages, their enthusiasm became infectious.

Brisk walking has now become very established throughout Singapore. Credit goes to my successor at Sembawang–Hong Kah CDC, Dr Teo Ho Pin who became CDC chairman in 2001. He took the ball and ran with it, expanding the number and scope of brisk walking groups greatly. When I relinquished my chairmanship to him, we had a chat. I listed some of the key programmes which I had started which I hoped he would continue to support. Expanding our brisk walking clubs or groups was right at the top. I am glad that he caught a glimpse of our vision too and did his best to pursue it. Inheriting 25 brisk walking clubs that had 1,400 members in 2001, he vigorously promoted it with the CDC staff in full support. By 2009, the number of clubs had expanded to 128 with 50,000 members. In September that year, it became a national programme when the Ministry of Community Development, Youth and Sports launched the National Brisk Walking Programme. Under this programme, People's Association received $1.9 million in over three years to work with the five

CDCs to implement and administer National Brisk Walking Clubs initiative, setting a target of 620 clubs and 100,000 members by 2012.[5] In that article, Ho Pin, co-chairman of this new initiative, was attributed to have set up the first brisk walking club in 2002. In fact, the first club was formed in 1998. By 2012, North West CDC had 128 clubs and 47,000 members.[6]

A second key CDC initiative was the "Maid-A-Friend" (MAF) programme, launched in May 2001. Ho Pin did not seriously pursue this initiative, unlike the brisk walking clubs, and it petered out after I relinquished chairmanship of the CDC. My motivation for doing this was to enhance the employer–maid relationship which I considered to be a critical one, especially with respect to the raising of young children.[7] My plan then was to develop the programme further after its launch, with a key mainstay of the programme being a voluntary half-day workshop which all first-time employers of foreign domestic workers would be encouraged to sign up for. I launched the programme in May 2001 at a workshop attended by 60 employers, saying that the workshop would cover issues such as "the nature of the employment relationship, the agent's role, the parties' roles, and responsibilities as well as the domestic workers' home lifestyle, values and mindset." I had earlier spoken to the then Minister for Labour (MOL)[8] on the need for such a workshop or session, hoping that MOL would make it mandatory for all first-time employers in Singapore. His view, as I recall it, was that there was no such need at that time. Hence, we proceeded to do it on our own at the CDC, on a non-compulsory basis. I felt that a voluntary workshop was at least a good start. Over time, if it proved useful, perhaps MOL would adopt the idea. I am happy that later on, the Ministry of Manpower decided to require first-time employers to undergo a session at the Ministry. I am sure that this move has made for a more conducive employer–maid relationship for many first-time employers. The workshop that we held was complemented by three other activities that were spaced out through the year. These were a "Making a Difference" or "MAD" Day, spearheaded by Heartware Network, where 200 National

Police Cadet Corp cadets distributed 2,000 goodie bags to 2,000 foreign domestic helpers congregated at an open field at Yishun who were enjoying a concert specially organised for them. The aim was to instil in our youths a sense of appreciation for the contribution of foreign workers in Singapore. On this, I am happy to see that many such efforts have proliferated in the past five to six years. Another event brought together employers with their children and their foreign domestic helpers working together on team-building games and sports as a family unit. Finally, we also organised a "Best Employer" competition which gave foreign domestic helpers an opportunity to express their appreciation to their employers by nominating them for the award. An encouraging number (67 good employers) were nominated. At the closing "Thank You" dinner in August that year, I said that "the two-month programme has achieved its purpose of highlighting the fact that both employers and employees can play a part in making the relationship work. Employers' relationship with their foreign domestic helpers is a special one. The foreign domestic helper lives in with her employer. They interact at close quarters..."

A third key initiative that the CDC seeded which has since evolved to benefit more Singaporeans is one that provided out-of-school youths and those at risk of leaving school prematurely with an opportunity to nurture non-academic skills, and to guide some back to school. This was "Project Bridge" launched in June 2000 as a collaboration between the CDC, YMCA, and the National Youth Council. A key concern behind this programme was that our system at that time was too rigid which tended to sideline the less academically-inclined ones. About one percent of the total school enrolment dropped out of primary and secondary schools each year then. Even though MOE had a programme to try to keep these students in the school system and the Institute of Technical Education (ITE) absorbed some of these school dropouts or early school leavers, quite a few were left to their own devices. The CDC interviewed some of these school dropouts who cited reasons such as "no interest in studies", "cannot cope in school", and "failed examinations" for their predicament. To me, there was a clear need to reach out to the annual cohort of school dropouts and others who were at risk of dropping out; hence, Project Bridge was conceived.

Before we initiated this project, I had spoken to the then Minister for Education[9] to express my concern for this group of students. I felt that more should be done to help develop their other innate non-academic interests and talents. This was because I believed, and still do, that everyone is unique and has something worthy to contribute to society. Some, especially when their strength was non-academic in nature, needed nurturing and affirmation. My recollection is that his response was that MOE was not quite prepared to create an alternative pathway for these school dropouts. If seen to be too readily available, it may cause more students to drop out; in other words, it may be seen as a "soft" option. This would be counter-productive to MOE's strenuous efforts to try to keep them within the school system. However, he was all for the idea of helping these students pursue their interests and passions through some other programme, which cheered my heart. I understood his concern as to why MOE could not create such a grand scheme, but felt that at the CDC level, we could initiate something to make a small difference. Perhaps, in time, our system would evolve to accommodate such an alternative scheme on an institutional basis. Hence, I am glad that we now have NorthLight School which provides hope to less academically-inclined students who nevertheless can have some formal education as well as nurturing of skills in a structured setting.[10] The Project Bridge Centre began operations in November 1999. At the time of its official launch in June 2000, 30 youths were participating in the centre's diverse activities that included games such as football, basketball and cycling; community service, camps and the imparting of important life skills such as using the computer, time management and effective decision-making. In my speech, I said:

> Activities at (this) Centre will nurture participating youths into whole persons and provide them with healthy ways and means to channel their energy. These activities seek to develop the social, vocational, academic, life and recreational skills of youths

so that they will lead productive lives. For example, a youth may not be interested in studies but is very interested in music... Likewise, a youth may be very interested in hairstyling... Youths who are keen to develop their vocational skills in servicing, mechanical or electronic fields will have an opportunity to do so through ITE's approved skills development programmee and joint partnership programmes with companies and institutions..."[11]

By December 2003, the centre had impacted the lives of about 550 youths. While all benefited from the life skills training, some became sufficiently motivated to seek re-admission to the school system, others continued with their education at YMCA's education centre, and yet others joined ITE. The remainder joined the workforce as productive workers. I remain grateful to YMCA for joining me in this novel venture. Later on, as the vision caught on, another centre with similar objectives, "180 degrees", spearheaded by Fei Yue, began operations. Even after NorthLight School's opening, Project Bridge and 180 degrees continued their outreach to less academically-inclined youths, as ground-up efforts to complement the School.

A fourth initiative which Sembawang–Hong Kah CDC incubated during my time as Chairman and which later grew into a national-level programme was the "Care and Support Programme for Offenders' Families". Under this initiative, grassroots leaders reached out to the families of inmates (normally the breadwinner) during the period of their incarceration. Launched in July 1998, I saw this outreach as one which grassroots leaders and community organisations were best-placed to undertake. For inmates who were prepared to link up with their families through this channel, it offered them an opportunity to express their love and continued concern for their loved ones who were left to fend for themselves. When launching the programme, I said that "CDC volunteers will help the family by providing emotional support, counselling, childcare and financial assistance. The early involvement of CDC volunteers can help prevent the breakdown of an offender's family." This expression of love and concern would in turn touch the family members, encouraging them not to give up on their incarcerated love ones, normally the father who was the family breadwinner. So while a wrongdoer serves time, which he or she must do, his/her links with the family would continue, albeit indirectly. We ran a pilot at one of the wards (Admiralty) in the District, under MP (Dr) Maliki Osman, calling it the "We Care" programme. He was a sociologist and was well-suited to the task, by training and temperament. Under his watchful and loving care, Maliki later expanded the programme to rope in suitable VWOs, such as family service centres, as part of a strengthened community support structure, where not only counselling but also concrete help could be extended. In time, the initial measures evolved into the Community Outreach Project (COP). With an established track record at Admiralty ward and with the Singapore Prisons Service's strong support, COP was expanded in 2010 to six wards.[12] As in the case of brisk walking clubs where Dr Teo Ho Pin is attributed to have started them, COP is attributed to the pioneering work of Dr Maliki Osman. This is not incorrect as he and his grassroots leaders indeed did the leg work on the ground. Still, the idea was conceived at our meetings at the Sembawang–Hong Kah CDC in the late 1990s, and was later launched and supported by the CDC.[13]

Another programme which has blossomed is one that helped the families of and children in preschools who were educationally challenged. This effort was channelled through the PAP Community Foundation (PCF) kindergartens, which I had charge of as Chairman of the PCF Executive Committee for 11 years from 1996 to 2007. In September 2011, the Ministry of Community Development, Youth and Sports made a significant announcement when it told *The Straits Times*[14] that it would be adding another 1,000 places to the Early Intervention Programme for Infants and Children (Epic) from 2011 to 2012. My heart cheered.

As early as 2004, the staff and I at PAP Community Foundation Headquarters (PCF HQ) had set up a small Special Educational Needs (SEN) team to look into what we felt was a pressing need, that is, pre-schoolers in the 130-odd PCF kindergartens with special learning and behavioural needs. In those days, PCF was easily the largest provider of kindergarten services in Singapore, holding a market share of about 70% of the children in each cohort. In part, I was inspired to push for this programme because of the early efforts of a PCF Clementi Branch kindergarten under MP Arthur Fong that had entered into a fruitful collaboration with the Canossian School for the Deaf. The School had sent staff to the kindergarten to teach a group of children with hearing impairment, helping them to integrate and interact with the other children in the normal classes.

The SEN team initiated a very modest pilot project at a few PCF kindergartens under which children who were identified to have developmental problems such as autism spectrum disorders, speech delays, and learning problems underwent some form of therapy. Hitherto, it was left very much to the discretion of each kindergarten's Principal. The more sympathetic ones tried their best to accommodate these children in their normal classes, making extra effort to ensure that these children did not disrupt class lessons. There were other kindergartens which also tried their best, unfortunately, to discourage the parents from sending their children to the kindergarten. At PCF HQ, we felt that these children and their parents deserved better. As long as the children's disability was manageable and treatable, they should receive specialist attention, and be guided and steered towards integrated learning with their peers. However, with PCF's principal goal of providing quality education at affordable costs to the bulk of Singaporeans living in our HDB estates, I had to tread carefully so that we would not nurture an albatross around our necks.

Thanks to the very dedicated SEN team at PCF HQ, we persevered, and delivered. Chief among my "collaborators" in the cause were Denise Low and Patricia Koh, who were specialists in the field, as well as PCF chief executive officer, Laura Khoo and her able deputy, Ruth Low. Lynda Ng was another longstanding loyal staff who looked after our finances. As we were very mindful of costs, we enlisted the support of philanthropic groups like the Lee Foundation in the initial years, and later the Lien Foundation. The Totalisator Board also chipped in. Working initially with the KK Women's and Children's Hospital and a few selected PCF centres whose supervisors caught a glimpse of the vision we shared,[15] we showed that with special attention, these children could cope and indeed, could in time be integrated with their peers in the classroom. Later in 2003, these children with special needs benefited from financial support given by the PCF Headstart Fund.[16] As the results were promising, over time, the programme was expanded to cover more centres. In 2009, it was further expanded to 22 PCF kindergartens in Pasir Ris–Punggol GRC as a further three-year pilot.[17] From an initial case referral volume of less than 100 cases per year in 2005, the SEN team was handling about 600 cases by 2011. As in other areas where we had made a modest start, I was happy to read a key recommendation in the Enabling Masterplan 2012–2016 put out by a steering committee appointed by MCYS for the establishment of a "network of early detection touch points in the community with the support of different stakeholders", and for the government to provide funding for "a nationwide developmental screening programme for children as young as nine months". These further measures are part of the scaffolding and framework supporting children with special needs, the foundation of which I believe the SEN team and I played a small part in laying.[18]

Another area where I hope I have made an enduring contribution is sports. Since young, I had believed in the positive impact of sports on a young person's development. Unabashedly, I had trumpeted the cause in many of my speeches, extolling the importance of co-curricular activities (CCA) in general, and sports in particular. Sports build up character and foster teamwork. Our students learn to be humble in winning and gracious in losing. They learn to persevere (through arduous training) and to strategise (as they play each game against different opponents). Mastering motor skills, they become more confident individuals. At primary school, I represented ACS at athletics (sprints, shot putt, long jump and 4×100-metre relay); Biddy Basketball (basketball played in a smaller court with a lower net) and badminton. At the secondary school level, I captained the football team, ran the low hurdles, and played rugby competitively for the school. Thus, having competed in both team games and in individual sports, I appreciated the different mindsets but similar rigorous mental training that each entailed. There is nothing like getting down to *ke garisan* (get to the lines) and then *sedia* (stand at the ready) with your arm muscles poised to explode — ready to spring, your legs ready to push out and your eyes looking in the distance at the row of hurdles lined up in front. Sometimes, you get to breast the tape as well, dipping your body into it! Contrast this with a delicate touch and "feign of the body" that beats your opponent, and then centering the football which meets the head of a teammate in the "six-yard box" who thumps it into the net. Each requires concentration and elicits elation of a different kind.

I met and courted my wife on the badminton court when she played competitively for the Singapore University (now, more than 60 years old, she still puts in two rigorous sessions weekly with a regular group of friends who have grown old together). Together with our three daughters, who are now 33, 29 and 24 years old, as a family, we had played a good spread of games for our schools, halls of residence, combined schools, and universities. These include badminton, basketball, handball, table tennis, netball, softball, football, touch rugby and athletics. When our children were young, my wife and I cycled, ran, swam, threw the frisbee and played many of the above games with them. Other than the ritual that most fathers go through — of teaching their young ones how to cycle — we had great fun when I also taught them how to kick a football, throw the shot-put and javelin, or shoot off the blocks in sprinting. At home, after dinner, we would play table tennis or pool. We are a very sporty family, where playing games together is a glue that has kept us close together all these years.

I contributed to sports at the national level via two channels: firstly, as Deputy Chairman of the Committee on Sporting Singapore (2000–2001) and secondly, as President of the

Football Association of Singapore (2004–2009). The Committee on Sporting Singapore (COSS) was formed in September 2000. Helmed by then Minister for Community Development and Sports, Mr Abdullah Tarmugi, with me as the Deputy Chairman and two Cabinet Ministers, Mr Mah Bow Tan and Mr Teo Chee Hean as Advisors, its brief was to draw up a new blueprint for Singapore sports to raise it to the next level.[19] It had wide representation[20] with a key focus to engage all the stakeholders meaningfully and sincerely. Split into four subcommittees on Strengthening the NSAs, Enhancing the Support Structure, Developing the Sports Industry and Improving the Environment for Community Bonding, it did not rush its work but proceeded steadily for more than a year. Its comprehensive report, which was well-received by the sporting fraternity and general public, embraced three key pillars — sports for all, sports industry and sports excellence, and projected six targets — getting started on a sturdy sports culture; creating a new sports environment; getting NSAs to be effective; implementing a "Sports for All" masterplan; promoting sports excellence including setting up a top-notch sports school and selling sports as a viable industry, including developing Singapore as an integrated sports hub. These three pillars and six targets in turn have become the key planks on which the sports renaissance which Singapore currently enjoys has been built on. There were detractors and sceptics when the Committee was first formed. After all, promoting sports and rolling out plans to lift sports was nothing new. Previous committees and earlier schemes had all endeavoured to do that. Some wondered whether this was another public relations exercise. In the words of the late Santokh Singh, a sports writer for *The New Paper* then, in his commentary on a forum held to present COSS' initial recommendations, *"I must admit that I started a sceptic... the press brief from COSS looked all too familiar... But I left the press conference a little more optimistic... Finally, there seems to be some direction for Singapore sports."*[21] Our report captured the mood of the day, including the pent-up passion in many sports-loving Singaporeans and administrators that Government should take a stronger lead to tap and channel the strong vein of interest out there. Many were waiting to spring into action. Indeed, "Passion" was the order of the day. I gave the Opening Address at the forum where I said:

> I am very encouraged by the passion and the huge amount of energy out there, waiting to be harnessed into a positive force for the good of sports in Singapore... No doubt, a challenge for us is to all work together to forge the diverse interests of the sporting fraternity into a clear, shared vision.

As reported in *The Straits Times* report the following day, "...And the 700 school principals, coaches, athletes, sports officials, students and parents responded passionately in turn at the feedback session."[22]

Today, our sports industry is humming along well. Singapore has organised many major international events and competitions in football, golf, tennis, rugby, table tennis, badminton, motor racing, sailing, cycling and swimming (among other sports). The Sports School has established a strong track record, both for turning out champions and also as a viable route for budding sports talents who also want a good academic education. The Singapore Sports Institute was recently launched. Many National Sports Associations have been re-energised and have produced many accolades for Singapore, at both regional and international games as well as their own respective world competitions. New NSAs of emerging sports are being formed. They continue to be manned by many committed volunteers who contribute expertise, sometimes money, and also sacrifice their time. Singapore won its first medal at the Olympics after a hiatus of 40 years when our table tennis girls did us proud at the Sydney Olympics Games in 2000 (Tan Howe Liang won a silver medal in weightlifting in Rome in 1960). Recently, at the Rio Olympics, Joseph Schooling won Singapore's very first Olympic gold medal, with Yip Pin Xiu, Laurentia Tan and Theresa Goh winning medals of all colours for Singapore at various Paralympics Games, including the 2016 edition. The "Sports for all" thrust has received renewed focus with school fields and halls being made available to public use through creative management schemes. Community sports has become the order of the day with the annual Singapore Community Games being a highlight. To the pleasant surprise of the Committee, Government in accepting the Report also committed a total outlay of $500 million over five years to implement all its proposals. To this, we have then PM Goh Chok Tong to thank. Mr Goh, being a keen sportsman himself,[23] appreciated the key role sports could play in uplifting the spirit of a nation, and was prepared to commit money to make it happen. Building on these strong foundations, it is good to see that then MCYS took sports to a higher level with the unveiling of its 'Vision for Sports' on 13 February 2011. Its 29 recommendations under the three thrusts of "To create more opportunities (where more Singaporeans of all ages will be involved in sports); "To improve access (where more Singaporeans — both able and disabled, by themselves or with friends and family members — can enjoy their sports in facilities specially designed for them); and "To deepen expertise (where our students will have enhanced opportunities to develop and further their interests and skills in sports). With the overall objective of making sports a part of the Singaporean lifestyle, these new initiatives have built on the momentum COSS generated and instil the strong values of sports in Singaporeans in direct and impactful ways.

Although I do my part in shaping policies and innovating measures, I am strongest on the ground as a hands-on person. One of my most fulfilling periods in politics is when I sat on the hottest seat in Singapore sports, as President of the Football Association of Singapore (FAS). Even though I had been involved in the FAS for many years before helming it,[24] the thrust into the seat came suddenly. This happened when then President, Mr Mah Bow Tan, who was also the Minister for National Development, felt the heavy weight of office when Singapore lost badly to Malaysia in the group stages of the Tiger Cup at our National Stadium, right before the eyes of 50,000 passionate fans. Mr Mah had by then already given 13 good years to local football, leading Singapore to a historic double in the Malaysia Cup and League in

1994, starting our very own S.League from scratch in 1996 when Singapore left the Malaysia Cup in unfortunate circumstances, and laying strong foundations for youth development by introducing a comprehensive National Football Academy (NFA) in 1999. He felt that the time had come to hand over to a younger, more energetic man. I was apprehensive but decided that the time had come for me to enter the arena as the point-man or striker for Singapore football. My abiding belief is that "football is not just another sport or marketing platform, but also a means to bond the community and to lift the spirits of Singaporeans, especially in these trying economic times."[25] When a country does well in football, especially in an extravaganza like the World Cup Finals which rivets the attention of the whole world, the spirit of the country soars. This was clearly demonstrated when hosts South Korea and Japan did well in the 2002 Finals.

I had a memorable time helming the FAS, ably supported by then FAS General Secretary John Koh and then S.League CEO Winston Lee, and volunteers in the FAS Council such as Tan Soo Nan, Lim Kia Tong and Lt-Gen (Rtd) Ng Jui Ping. Singapore football also owes a debt of gratitude to the late Kwek Leng Joo who gamely took on the onerous task of being the founding chairman of the fledgeling S.League in 1995 at Mr Mah's request at short notice. Undergirding the S.League clubs as volunteer chairmen in the early years were stalwarts like Teo Hock Seng, Patrick Ang, John Yap and S Thevaneson. They, and many others, were "Friends of Football".[26] Of course, we were also grateful for the many fans who supported local football, chief of whom was none other than our then President, the late Mr SR Nathan. President Nathan showed a warm sincerity in supporting local football, not only when we were up but also when we were down. He came not only for the "big games", but for other games as well. A memorable game that he and Mrs Nathan came to support was one between two ladies' teams played at one of our smaller sports stadia. What has stayed in my mind is that of Mrs Nathan standing up to cheer when one of the players scored a good goal from outside the box! And all of us, including President Nathan, stood up as well!

When I stepped down after five years in March 2009, the media was generous in describing these five years as "five successful years (when) football went through a period of growth and success",[27] and "an era where Singapore football has enjoyed tremendous success."[28] Key achievements included two consecutive ASEAN championships,[29] Singapore's best showing in the World Cup qualifiers,[30] the SEA Games Under-23 team went beyond the group stages and won a bronze medal for the first time, the S.League was named by the Asian Football Confederation as one of Asia's top 10 Leagues in 2008, paving the way for the SAF Football Club (the Warriors) to participate in the top tier of Asian club football, the AFC Champions League,[31] and for the first time since George Suppiah in 1974, a Singaporean, Shamsul Maidin was appointed by FIFA to officiate at the World Cup Finals. At the FAS' 2009 Annual General Meeting when I announced my stepping down, I said that I had achieved most of what I had set out to do which I had detailed in a five-year FAS Roadmap shortly after I became President in April 2004.

After assuming office, I thought long and hard about what I should do to stem the slide in local football. Key was winning back the support of Singaporeans for local football. A bugbear then was FAS' declared goal of securing a place in the final rounds of the World Cup, encapsulated in the catchphrase, "GOAL 2010". Mr Mah had announced this in 2000 to rally Singaporeans to the cause by focusing on a specific objective, that is, to get into the Finals. He wanted to achieve a mindset change in Singaporeans. The 2010 timeframe was added not so much as a specific target that must be achieved to determine success, but to strongly kick-start the process of getting there. Perhaps, 10 to 11 years was too ambitious, but in football, nothing is impossible. If it had been Goal 2014, 14 to 15 years may not provide such a strong impetus to kick-start the process and galvanise Singaporeans. The problem that I pondered deeply over when I took over as President was this — with us staring imminently at the "2010" time frame, and with most Singaporeans mocking the FAS for being unrealistic in view of our 4–0 loss to Malaysia, what could and should I do to retain the objective but also regain Singaporeans' support?

Goal 2010, although well-intended, had become an albatross around the FAS' neck!

I gave a press conference a month or so into my Presidency to set out my goals. As the date loomed closer, I was still grappling with this key issue which I knew the media would surely press for an answer. Two weeks or so before D-Day, as I worked on my talking points, a flash of inspiration came. I decided I would produce a one-page Roadmap that would set out various targets for local football. One of these would be to get to the World Cup; that would remain an objective, but it need not be in 2010. As there were four other targets, the focus would not be on this reorientation, which some critics would argue was a shifting of the goalpost. At the press conference, I knew I had to dispassionately explain why Mr Mah had initiated Goal 2010 in the first place, and that it had succeeded in galvanising Singaporeans to the cause; for example, a new National coach, Raddy Abramovic, with good credentials had been appointed; a National Youth Academy with solid plans had been launched by PM; our Foreign Talent Scheme was in place and a few promising foreign talents had been inducted. The work had just begun. We would not get there by 2010 but one day, 2018 or more likely 2022, we may get there!

The Roadmap became the blueprint for the five years of football renaissance that followed. Other than the reorientation of GOAL 2010, our targets were to build up the S.League as one of the best in Asia; to connect with the ground and foster community spirit; to groom young local talent and for football to be part of a vibrant sports industry. At the time of my stepping down, I felt these targets were largely met.

What are some enduring memories from my time as FAS President? First, my many events and functions on the ground, especially those that involved young footballers playing "small" five- or seven-a-side games. These were held not only at Jalan Besar stadium, but all over Singapore in open fields such as Marine Parade and West Coast Park. Their faces, as well as those of their enthusiastic and proud parents, will remain forever etched in my mind. I will also remember my very first "President's

Tea" held in July 2004, three months or so after I assumed office. I wanted to show that FAS was sincere in hearing its fans out. We wanted to know their views and suggestions. We were interested in tapping the expertise of volunteers. Hence, FAS extended an open invitation online to anyone who wanted to drop by to have a chat with me on a Saturday afternoon at Jalan Besar. At that inaugural session, about 25 people came, representing diverse backgrounds which included parents, school coaches, recreational league administrators and fans, both "die-hard" and sceptical ones. As reported in TODAY,[32] the scheduled one and half hour session extended to three hours, a "testament to the level of concern for the game". I was quoted as saying: "It was a fruitful session with views from a wide range of people from different backgrounds. The linkage between the FAS and volunteers and friends of football is an important one and it was good to hear many different views and suggestions from the people on the ground." Two quotes by those who came were: "Prof Ho is doing the right thing by opening up the issues in Singapore football for a public dialogue session",[33] and "Today was a good start and an important step for Singapore football".[34]

In all, we held about five such sessions. Nearer the field of play, I will never forget jumping for joy when Khairul Amri scored our equaliser in a "must draw" game at Bangkok's National Stadium on 4 February 2007 in the finals of the ASEAN Federation Cup (successor to the Tiger Cup). We had won the first-leg in Singapore and could not afford to lose in Bangkok. My getting to attend the game was already not a given, as there were some political tensions during that time between Singapore and Thailand. I had consulted MFA whether I should fly to Bangkok to watch the game and decided, almost at the last minute, that I would go. Even then, MFA felt that it would be safer to assign me a security officer. So, with SO Fong accompanying me, we made the trip and joined almost 30,000 passionate Thai fans at the stadium. To the credit of our Thai hosts and fans, the game was played in a competitive but sporting atmosphere. At no time did I feel uneasy, both inside and outside the stadium. In fact, I felt so at home and absorbed into the atmosphere of the occasion that I unabashedly jumped for joy and shouted when Khairul Amri scored our equaliser, much to the discomfort and chagrin of my Thai hosts seated around me! Khairul had gone on a mazy run from near the halfway line. He then unleashed a mighty kick just outside the penalty box that took a wicked last-minute curve right into goal. That is me, always wearing my feelings on my sleeves.

Yet another memorable moment was when on separate occasions after our victorious Tiger Cup and AFF Cup campaigns, Aide and Indra[35] handed me a Championship medal. These, as well as visits to Amara Hotel, where our Lions set up camp for home matches on these campaigns, when I spoke to them to rouse their spirits, remain moments to treasure. While there were exhilarating moments in football, football also created a very low point in my political career. This happened in 2006 when I was attacked in the media for being soft on a foreign-born Singaporean player who had disappeared for several weeks after signing up with an Indonesian club and being paid a handsome sign-on fee.[36] He re-appeared after some time with the explanation that he had travelled to far-flung places, such as Russia, to try to secure employment on better terms with a club elsewhere. He explained that, while away, he could not get in touch with his new Indonesian club management to let them know where he was. FAS meted out punishment which some fans and a local newspaper considered way too soft. The newspaper criticised me, as FAS President, for endorsing wrongdoing! I felt really down at that time as I felt that my judgement (even though it was in the area of football), as an office-holder in Ministries that promoted law and order in Singapore, was being impeached! Thankfully, after a few weeks, the flood of criticisms passed.

While one of my first acts was to reach out to sceptical fans through the President's Tea, my very last act before I stepped down at the AGM on 30 March 2009 was to lift the ban on all football activities imposed on Abas Saad since 1995. Those of us in our 40s and 50s will remember Abas as being a key member of the Lions in the early 1990s. He had, together with key players like Fandi, Sundram, and Alistair Edwards (another Australian), helped Singapore achieve a momentous double in 1994 when Singapore won both the FAM premier league as well as the Malaysia Cup. In June, 1995, he was found guilty by the courts in Singapore of helping then teammate Michal Vana to fix matches in the FAM Premier League competition. Abas had played a minor role in the conspiracy, agreeing to do what he was supposed to do, that is, to score goals. He did not receive any money and pulled out of the arrangement after three matches. He was fined $50,000. As early as 2005 or thereabouts, through the good office of his strike partner Fandi, Abas had met me to plead his case. He said his heart was very much with Singapore football and wanted to be able to contribute to its cause. I could sense his sincerity and deep desire to immerse himself once again in football activities here. Nevertheless, because Singapore takes a tough stand against corruption of any sort, I treaded carefully. Abas had continued playing football in Australia and then turned to coaching after hanging up his boots. His expertise was in youth development, something we also emphasised in Singapore. By the 2008 AGM, FAS had considered his case and was prepared to lift the ban. Still, as FAS President and Senior Minister of State of Law and Home Affairs, I was very mindful that the timing and presentation of the reasons for our move was critical. With a surge in corruption allegations in the S.League emerging around that time, I decided to hold back. I had one year to reconsider. By the time of the 2009 AGM, I was convinced that, examining all the circumstances of the case, it was indeed the right thing to do. I was prepared to respond to any unhappiness that may surface at what some may see as FAS' softening on corruption. As it turned out, the announcement on the lifting of Abas' suspension was met with muted response. In fact, whatever response it elicited was more positive than negative. After all, 15 years had lapsed since the ban. Abas was still remembered by some for his football exploits, especially as Fandi's strike partner. He had also never run Singapore football down over this long period. Personally, I am happy for him as Abas was indeed one of football's early foreign talent who had immersed well with the local footballers and fans.

My one big regret in running the FAS is not building and operating futsal centres. Now, there are many commercially-run ones which are doing well. As FAS President, I had officiated at many futsal and street soccer events, playing at quite a number myself. The turnout would invariably be very good. A prime advantage of futsal over field football is that it is an "all-weather" activity. All you need are six to eight friends to organise themselves after a hard day's work to come and sweat it out.[37] If the location is easily accessible and the charges reasonable, the enterprise would be successful. If I had done this, it would have given FAS a constant income stream. It would also have enabled FAS to visibly "fly its flag" among football-loving Singaporeans and gain some goodwill by helping them to have their regular "fix".

There is much that I can share about Singapore football. Thankfully, the National Archives of Singapore (NAS) felt this way too. In May, 2009, I had three sessions with Mr Mohamad Yussoff Ahmad, a very experienced interviewer with the NAS Oral History Centre. They lasted, in total, about five to six hours where I shared freely on Singapore football. These musings are now part of our oral history, available at the National Archives of Singapore. Still, football is always work in progress. Whoever is FAS President, my ardent hope is that Singaporeans will support him and especially our various national teams (at different levels), and our very own S.League which is an important component of our football ecosystem. May the new National Stadium reverberate with a reenergised "Kallang Roar"!

Today, I remain active in supporting sports. On retiring from politics, I remained as FAS Advisor and became Chief Patron of Singapore Athletics (SA). For the latter post, SA's then President, Tang Weng Fei, had asked me to lend a hand. I agreed because Weng Fei had readily agreed to help out at a S.League club in the 1990s when I needed someone with commitment, energy, and financial resources to step up to the plate. Some will remember Weng Fei as a national hurdler in the 1970s. In fact, we had represented ACS in the low hurdles over 80-metres when we were in Secondary 2 as 14-year-old teenagers. If I remember correctly, we were the second- and third-best in Singapore then. Weng Fei will be the first to say (which he still does today) that I had taught him how to hurdle properly. He had the height and power; I had the technique and style! This is one example in my life where friendships have come a long way (and there are many other examples), and where like stone rubbing stone, we have rubbed off "good works" on each other to benefit a larger whole.

I have many friends like this. Some were peers who played a part in shaping my life. Some were from ACS; others from NJC; yet others from my National Service period or law studies. A precious few had helped me to navigate through difficult periods of my life such as times when relationships were lost or disrupted. Others were instrumental in helping me cement key relationships such as my courtship period leading to my marriage! I cherish friendships and value these "Friends for Life".

What about my "extra-curricular activities" or ECAs? Heading the list will be as Advisory Board member in the early days of the National Youth Achievement Award (NYAA) when Dr Tay Eng Soon headed the organisation. NYAA is the local operating partner of the Duke of Edinburgh Award scheme that had worldwide reach. Being an established and reputable scheme that reached out to all segments of a student cohort (not just the academically bright students), it was a scheme worth supporting as a political office-holder has always chaired the Board of Advisors. When Dr Tay passed on, Mr Mah Bow Tan took over. In turn, Mr Mah handed the baton to Mr Heng Swee Keat, Minister for Finance. Installed as Board member in 1992, it gave me great pleasure to officiate at many events to affirm students who had completed the various stages of the Award (bronze, silver, and gold) fulfilling requirements in the areas of community service, leadership, and adventure. As MHA office-holder, I am glad that I had played a part in paving the way for the NYAA scheme to be introduced to inmates in the Prisons' School. This had appeared formidable at first as it was difficult for the participants to satisfy the requirement of adventure. A way out came when NYAA settled for overnight camping conducted in a secure setting on the prisons' grounds, a creative modification and application of the criterion! Since the Prisons Service's adoption of the NYAA programme in 2000, nearly 1,500 young inmates have taken part in it.[38]

Another key youth organisation I was actively involved in was Heartware Network (HWN), which I launched in the year 2000. HWN is a ground-up initiative that seeks to nurture youth voluntarism, entrepreneurship, and leadership development. It was started by an idealistic young man moved to action by then PM Goh's call for a stronger focus to be put on creating a stronger "heartware" in Singaporeans. Raymond Huang was then a young banker, stationed in Shanghai.[39] Stirred by the call, he left his secure banking job to found HWN. HWN has a large database of youth volunteers built up over the years of its active involvement in key national events such as the National Day Parade and Chingay procession. It has a particular focus on less academically-inclined students, seeking to inspire them to discover themselves and do well in life in every sense of the word.[40] One of its arms, Youth Business Singapore (YBS), is the national operating entity of Youth Business International (YBI), an organisation spanning more than 20 countries founded by Prince Charles. Today, Tan See Leng is HWN's hardworking Executive Director. Finally, out of the many other "ECAs" that I undertook, involving diverse interests such as Chinese opera,[41] Chinese traditional medicine,[42] my own clan association,[43] and homes for the intellectually-disabled and for senior citizens, I will highlight just one more hat that I wore — as Patron of the Children's Cancer Foundation (CCF).

CCF had started as Working in Aid of Leukemic Kids (WALK) in 1992. WALK was started by a group of fresh graduates, key among whom was a newly-minted medical doctor, Tan Hiang Khoon, who became WALK's founding President. He was well supported by a few other fresh graduates who were key office-holders of the Junior Common Room Committees of the various NUS Halls of Residence in the late 1980s. They included Gregory Vijayendran, Wong Poey Yong, Carolyn Ng, and Christina Kheng. In addition to being Hall President, Gregory was also very much involved in Camp Rainbow. When I was Master of Kent Ridge Hall (KR) from 1988 to 1993, the Hall hosted a group of children suffering from cancer under the Camp Rainbow outreach. Earlier on, they had encountered difficulty in securing a venue for the five-day camp. When I learnt of their predicament and was approached to host the camp, I agreed readily, but only after I had consulted the elected student leaders of the Hall (the Junior Common Room Committee). This was because there were unfounded fears circulating at that time, which had apparently turned off prospective hosts who were approached. One was the safety of the children (whether the Hall would be embroiled in any dispute should any child get hurt or became ill). Worse, some held silly fears that the children's stay in the student rooms (this was during vacation time when the rooms were empty) would put off future users of the room (as the children were ill and their illness could be infectious). If so, this may afflict future users of the room. To the credit of student leaders in Kent Ridge Hall's JCRC at that time, they stood with me. We agreed that we must do our part for these children. In 1996, when WALK was renamed CCF, the committee approached me to become its Patron. I readily agreed as I wanted to affirm this group of student leaders who had volunteered their time and expertise during a phase of their lives when many of their peers were busy pursuing their careers or other interests, including courting prospective spouses. CCF has grown from strength to strength through the years. Today, it hosts a widely supported "Hair for Hope" annual fund-raiser that enables supporters and donors to identify with children stricken with cancer through the shaving of hair. In addition, my family is supportive of cancer causes.

My father, a successful self-made businessman who built up a lucrative watch retail business from scratch, had died of colorectal cancer a few days short of turning 50 in 1973 (I was then doing my NS undergoing the Officer's Cadet Course). Out of eight siblings, three have been afflicted with cancer, with two deaths resulting. I will turn 63 in May this year and thank God for every day that I live. Till today, I remain Patron of CCF.

I have no regrets that I lived my life fully as an all-rounder!

Lessons in Leadership

1 Leading with passion is very important. If you are not passionate about doing something, think twice about doing it. Enthuse the ground and those whom you work with with your passion! Your passion comes through when you "walk the talk" and roll up your sleeves to be "one of the boys". Join in what the others are doing, whether it is participating in a treasure hunt, quiz or telematch. Do not just be "the boss" or Guest-of-Honour, cheering politely from the sidelines; join in, and do so wholeheartedly!

2 Never be discouraged when your "bosses" do not take up your suggestions or causes. Understand where they are coming from. It could be a matter of time and/or a question of available resources at that time. If you are convinced that your suggestion or idea is indeed good for the organisation, you may try to achieve your heart-felt objectives without undermining their positions; for example, try out a smaller scale "pilot scheme" first or adjust your plan to address their concerns. Adapt and scale up later if feasible. Do not just show your unhappiness and give up! In doing so, bring other partners on board. When others join you, they show support for your idea and affirm you as "partner". It is an expression of confidence.

3 Life is to be lived fully. As a leader, as you espouse this belief in your life, it will rub off on others too. While we seek to be the best that we can be in our chosen profession, there is so much out there in life to be explored and experienced. Look beyond the confines of what you do for a living during the workday or your comfort zone, to stretch yourself and realise your full potential as a person. Enjoy life; enjoy people; enjoy yourself! Immerse yourself in sports, the arts, hobbies or travelling with family or friends (especially the free-and-easy kind where you plan the itinerary yourself, book everything yourself and travel around independently in a rented car or on trains and such).

Endnotes

1. In NJC and my Law class at the Singapore University, my peers recognised that I was an "all-round" student. I think I have won this "award" several times! In my studies, while I have generally done well (within the top two to five percent banding of the class), I have never topped the class except in Primary 5 at ACS when, somehow, I topped the standard which had 218 students (not sure how I did it though!) At the University, I was second in a graduating class of about 130 students. For my 'A' levels, I had a "AABB" scorecard with a 'One' in General Paper. Being from an Arts class, I believe that I would have been among the top Arts students in my cohort that year. This is because I have always set aside time for my extra-curricular activities (ECA). I believe in stretching myself and living life fully, not to only focus on one area of endeavour (whether it be studies or work).
2. I was the youngest finalist that year. Other finalists who were more accomplished than me then included Zainul Abidin Rasheed (who later became Senior Minister of State), Raymond Chia (several years my senior in ACS and a SAF captain at that time) and John Ang (a NUS social work lecturer who later was a fellow Resident Fellow at Kent Ridge Hall). Even in those early years, our lives were interlinked! Prime Minister Lee Hsien Loong won the Award two years before me in 1972.
3. Sembawang Town Council General Manager Soon Min Sin was a great help.
4. At that time, in the late 1990s, there was no focus on integrating recent immigrants into Singapore society. As it has turned out, brisk walking has become a key activity by which new immigrants, especially the older folks from the PRC, have mixed with the local community.
5. See *The Sunday Times*, 18 October 2009, p. 9.
6. In 2001 after the May General Elections, five mayors were appointed to head five newly-configured CDCs based on the new electoral boundaries. Before then, the five CDCs were headed by two mayors and three chairmen, of whom I was one. Sembawang–Hong Kah CDC was reduced in land size and became North West CDC.
7. In 2001, my three girls were 18, 14, and nine years old. Since my oldest girl was born, we have had domestic helpers from the Philippines help raise them. As my wife, who was a lawyer in

practice, never stopped working, their help was critical. Having had them live with us over these 18 years, we appreciated the need for both employer and maid to understand the dynamics at work. This was especially true of the employer who would normally have the upper hand in the relationship.
8. It is now called the Ministry of Manpower. The Minister then was Dr Lee Boon Yang.
9. The Minister at that time was Mr Teo Chee Hean, now DPM.
10. Recounting the setting up of NorthLight in 2007, then Minister for Education Heng Swee Keat in a COS speech in Parliament in 2012 said that when MOE set up NorthLight School, it was "both a bold innovation and also a leap into the unknown".
11. The centre's pioneer corporate sponsors who came on board in its first year of operations despite the centre not having a proven track record included Groupe Danone, Deutsche Bank, Guardian SEA, Khong Guan Biscuits, Lucent Technologies, Nestle, Nike, the Netherlands Embassy, Pacific Internet, Pasta Fresco da Salvatore Restaurant, Pearson Education, Schwan Stabilo, Shell Singapore, and Singapore Press Holdings.
12. These were Tampines West, Kaki Bukit, Marsiling, Nanyang, Taman Jurong, and Thomson.
13. In my last public speech as an office-holder at the Prisons-SCORE conference on 29 March 2011, interestingly, I mentioned the Community Outreach Programme.
14. See *The Straits Times*, 25 September 2011, Prime p. 8.
15. I remain grateful to these early pioneers in the field.
16. The Headstart Fund was another channel started when I was PCF Exco chairman to help disadvantaged children in Singapore. The Fund assists young Singaporeans from disadvantaged families (aged four to 10) to have a headstart in life through a good grounding in their early years in education. Each child who is assisted would also have a volunteer from the local community as friend and mentor.
17. See *The Straits Times*, 7 July, p. B3.
18. See *TODAY*, 22 February 2012, front page.
19. CoSS had four objectives: (1) establish the vision and desired outcomes for sports; (2) identify the issues impeding the development of sports; (3) formulate the development strategies for sports; and (4) recommend specific initiatives for the future development of sports.

20. Its members hailed from the National Sports Associations, media, private sector, grassroots, the schools and Singapore Pools.
21. *The New Paper*, 23 February, 2001, p. 62.
22. *The Sunday Times*, 25 February, p. 46.
23. Mr Goh swam competitively for the Raffles Institution as a student. As an adult, he is a keen golfer and tennis player.
24. I was approached to be FAS President as early as 1995 when Mr Teo Chong Tee stepped down. I consulted Prof Jaya and Mr Wong Kan Seng, both of whom felt that I should concentrate on my Ministry duties as I was relatively new in the job. That was sound advice which I am glad I took. Later in 1997, I became FAS Second Adviser and then Deputy President in 1999 when Mr Mah Bow Tan, then Minister for National Development relinquished his position as FAS Advisor and took over the hot seat as President. In those days, FIFA accepted our explanation as to why FAS Exco office-holders and members were appointed by the Government. FIFA did not exert any pressure for FAS to hold elections for these positions.
25. This was my quote reported by *The Straits Times* when I stepped down in March, 2009 (*The Straits Times*, 25 March 2009, p. B11.)
26. This was my opening salutation at all football events — "FOF" to signify the closeness of our footballing fraternity and our shared destiny.
27. *The Straits Times*, 25 March p. B11.
28. *TODAY*, 25 March p. 32.
29. The first was winning the Tiger Cup in 2005 and the second was winning the ASEAN Football Championship in 2007.
30. The Lions battled their way valiantly into the third round of the qualifiers for the first time.
31. That was rarified atmosphere where our top local club competed with top Japanese, Korean and Chinese teams.
32. *TODAY*, 5 July, 2004, p. 42.
33. By pilot Leow Yoong Pyng, a die-hard S.League fan.
34. By Hari Das who ran a recreational soccer league.
35. They were the skippers of the two squads that did us proud at the Tiger Cup and AFF Cup campaigns.
36. Agu Casmir hailed from Nigeria and was one of our earlier foreign players inducted under the Foreign Talent Scheme. He had played a pivotal role when we won the Tiger Cup in 2005.

37. This is not unlike how squash was a convenient outlet to destress in the past!
38. See the *The Straits Times*, 24 April 2015.
39. This was before OUB merged with UOB.
40. In June 2011, shortly after I left political office, I agreed to be Heartware Network's Advisor to affirm them in their important work of reaching out to Singapore's youths.
41. I was Patron of the Chinese Opera Society in the early years and later, assumed the chairmanship of the Kreta Ayer People's Theatre Management Committee. I believe that Chinese opera as an art form holds out important values for our young such as loyalty to country, devotion to family, patience and perseverance, and filial piety. It also has interesting techniques in singing and movement. As Master of Kent Ridge Hall in 1993, I had persuaded the hall students to forego the traditional annual "Starburst" (a cultural extravaganza of songs and dance normally of the modern, western genre) for that year to instead stage an "Operaburst". To the credit of the students, they were game and learnt what they needed to know about Chinese Opera under diva Hong Hong, a Fulbright Scholar and daughter of the famous Hongxian Nu. A fringe event of the 1993 Festival of Asian Performing Arts, 50 students of various races performed four excerpts taken from "Six Kingdoms Jointly Appoint a Prime Minister", "Cun Cao the Witty Maid", "Sun Wukong Battles the White Bone Spirit", and "Ode to Liche" as a joint performance with the Chinese Opera Society (see *The Straits Times*, 21 September 1993). I also officiated at several performances of the Chinese Opera Institute helmed by Dr Chua Soo Pong.
42. I had close links with the Chung Hwa Free Clinic after they established a clinic in Nee Soon East. Contrary to what some may think, I was no "banana" — yellow on the outside and white inside. In fact, having spent two years of preschool (when I was only five and six years old) at Kum Yan Methodist Church kindergarten, I was well-grounded in Chinese, both as a language and as a value system. Hence, unlike most of my 'O' level classmates in ACS in 1970, I scored a B3 for my Chinese, something I am proud of.
43. I followed in my father's footsteps by being active in Ho See Seng Tong after I took on political office. I felt it was my filial duty to do so. Moreover, I had benefited from the clan association's generosity in my earlier years of schooling, having received a bursary from it.

Chapter 6 | # THE 2001 GENERAL ELECTIONS

Amidst all this talk, the man who mattered most, Assoc Prof Ho, refused to buckle, dismissing the bookies' prediction as nothing more than rumour-mongering. "They don't have the finger on the people's pulse," he said. "I know them (the residents). They know me. Young children come up to me and say "Hello, Uncle Ho, I shook hands with you when I was in kindergarten," and grown-ups come and wish me good luck. I've been here 10 years. I've put my heart and soul into my work. I've turned this place into one which we can be proud of. I promise to make it even better. There is no reason why the contest should be close, let alone why I should lose... On the eve of Polling Day, he gave a stirring speech, putting in detail his track record... "The question now is: Ho Peng Kee or Poh Lee Guan. It's my track record against his. The choice is clear," were his final words.

Asked to describe his battle, he said, "Exciting, interesting... it was a good experience. I've learnt a lot. It has definitely made me a better politician. It's always great to come in with a people's mandate."

TODAY, 5 November 2001

I don't take it personally. I take it in the spirit of electioneering, rumours flying around in the heat of a campaign. What's important is, you must feel what you're doing is right.

The New Paper, 11 August 2005

I suppose it was how the issue was being built up in the media," he said. Sometimes, you need good 'election stories' during the polls. Even on my walkabouts prior to polling day, some residents were asking me what exactly was the problem and many of them felt that nothing was amiss. That was what I sensed as well. In fact, I told the political leaders who came that there was nothing to worry about and that I would stand on my track record in Nee Soon East. So, even though there was a storm created, to me, it was a storm in a teacup.

TODAY, 20 October 2005

The 2001 General Elections

It was my opportunity to shine, to show everyone that I could stand on my own and win decisively. This included the party leadership who had enough faith in me so as to carve out Nee Soon East as a single-member constituency (from Sembawang GRC).[1] Then DPM Tony Tan said as much when he pulled me aside in the Nomination Centre on Nomination Day. Walking a few paces with me, I remember him saying, to the effect, that if I did not want to remain a Minister of State all of my political life, this was my opportunity to shine. Galvanised and encouraged, I was all ready to fight a good fight and win decisively.

In fact, very early on, I was all ready to fight a General Election (GE) campaign, whether as part of a GRC or as a single ward. For 10 years, I had worked the ground assiduously. As I had shared in Chapter 1, I adopted an informal and interactive style, shaking hands wherever I went in Nee Soon East, greeting residents and getting to know them and their children. We had many well-attended large-scale events, and my Meet the People sessions (MPS) were always packed. On average, I met about 70 residents each week at my MPS, with about one-third of them being new cases. In other words, over the course of 10 years, I would have helped about 12,000 residents.[2] Through the Town Council, I had built many facilities in the constituency. I had also introduced key services, such as the Chung Hwa Free Clinic and a Student Care Service Centre. I was ready for a good GE campaign! Alas, things went awry.

The writing was on the wall when one of our newspapers, in covering Nomination Day, quite unfortunately, painted me as a political novice. I recall feeling uncomfortable then as I felt it was not a complimentary picture. The report said that, in fighting my first election, I could rely on fellow MP Ong Ah Heng, a veteran grassroots man for help. It highlighted me asking him what he would be doing after filing his nomination papers. I do not recall our exact conversation although I do recall speaking with him, since we were both Single Member Constituencies (SMCs) and were located next to each other.[3] I could very well have asked him what was reported.

Still, it was unfortunate that the paper took that slant, especially as a fierce campaign was expected in all the SMCs. The contrast that some people may have drawn was that Ah Heng was a seasoned "coffee shop" politician who spoke Hokkien fluently and connected well with residents, while I was an English-speaking, urbane, rookie campaigner unsure of how to fight the campaign. Of course, these caricatures often do not tell the full story.

Other than the fact that I was fighting my first political campaign (having received two walkovers as part of Sembawang GRC helmed by then DPM Tony Tan in the 1991 and 1996 GEs), the other noteworthy feature of the 2001 GE campaign in Nee Soon East, which the media later dubbed as one of three hot seats in the GE, was the fact (not often mentioned) that the Workers' Party (WP) had poured resources initially dedicated to a GRC, into Nee Soon East. Indeed, other than Hougang SMC, where MP Low Thia Khiang was defending his seat, the only other seat which the Workers' Party ultimately contested that year was Nee Soon East! This came about because the Workers' Party team slated to contest Aljunied GRC was disqualified during the Nomination process as their papers were found not to be in order. Hence, the candidates in the Workers' Party Aljunied team were re-deployed to Nee Soon East; for example, the WP held three rallies over the nine-day campaign period in Nee Soon East. On the ground, I recall seeing the intended Aljunied GRC candidates on many occasions campaigning for its candidate for Nee Soon East, Dr Poh Lee Guan. Other than just numbers and the logistical support extended, I am sure that the frustration at being disqualified on Nomination Day itself, when one is all mentally psyched up for battle, would have resulted in a swelling of greater determination shown by the disqualified candidates and their supporters. This difference was palpable as I compare the intensity of the Workers' Party campaign in 2001 and 2006, when Dr Poh Lee Guan contested against me again in Nee Soon East SMC.

The campaign was unexceptional during the first three to four days. Like other PAP candidates, I visited residents at their homes, shook hands at the market, coffee shops and eating places, and distributed flyers and brochures at the bus stops and MRT stations. On the fifth day (Monday), then Senior Minister Lee (hereafter referred to as "Mr Lee"), while meeting reporters after a visit to Tampines GRC, said that he had heard that the odds at Nee Soon East had evened out to 50–50, from the original odds of "eight to nine in favour of PAP".[4] He qualified this, saying that "bookmakers (the illegal bookies that operate on the ground at every GE) judge by the "crowds and the pyrotechnics" at opposition rallies. I don't think it's that simple."[5] The following day (Tuesday), PM Goh, referring to the 50–50 odds at Nee Soon East, was reported to have dismissed such "betting and coffee shop talk" as being influenced by rumours, and said he was confident of victory in Nee Soon East.[6] Still, warning bells sounded at PAP HQ that trouble might be brewing in Nee Soon East, as intelligence gathered on the ground indicated that a poison letter targeting a key Nee Soon East grassroots leader was circulating, alleging unethical business practices and wrongdoing. When I read the report from HQ, I must say that I was very disturbed as this matter had, for me, gone below the radar. I knew that there was some rumbling against this grassroots leader whose business had not gone well, resulting in some of his clients and customers who had invested with him being unhappy. I had considered the matter and treated it as a matter of legitimate business failure, with no wrongdoing involved. In fact, my understanding was that this matter had been looked into by the authorities and no further actions had been taken. I must say, however, that knowledge of the incipient ground unhappiness and rumours affected my mental state, as quite a few people commented later that I looked troubled and tired during the hustings. It was the realisation of this oversight on my part dawning on me rather than the fear of losing the GE that made me look tired.

Notwithstanding the brewing storm, I remained confident that I would win, and win well. As I shared quite a few times with well-meaning Party leaders who were concerned, and also with the media, I knew that my 10 years of close interaction with my residents would be the litmus test, not rumours or unhappiness expressed against any grassroots leader. As reported in *The New Paper*, I said that "I expect(ed) to win 60% of the vote."[7] As it turned out, I scored a resounding 73.8% win, helped by a strong overall electoral performance by the PAP. So much for the bookie's odds![8] As the 2015 GE have clearly shown, these odds are totally unreliable. In fact, they can be swayed by arbitrary factors, not least a disgruntled bettor placing a huge bet against a candidate to lower the odds against him winning. Who knows — this could have been my case in 2001!

TODAY reported me as refusing "to buckle, dismissing the bookies' prediction as nothing more than rumour-mongering". They cast me in a defiant mood, saying: "They (the bookies) don't have the finger on the people's pulse. I know them (the residents). They know me... There is no reason why the contest should be close, let alone why I should lose."[9] Indeed, I stood firmly on my track record, captured not just in brick and mortar but, more importantly, in touched lives and warm handshakes. In my interactions throughout the nine days of campaigning, residents remained very warm. Many assured me that, notwithstanding media reports that said my campaign was in trouble, they were solidly behind me. In fact, what was really heart-warming were the assurances of support expressed by families living in close proximity to each other, all in Nee Soon East. Thus, residents would not only say that they would vote for me but that their siblings, also living in the constituency, would vote for me too. In my rally speech on the night before voting began, I was reported to have given "a stirring rally speech, putting in detail (my) track record..." I ended my rally speech with this question posed to Nee Soon East's voters: "The question now is — Ho Peng Kee or Poh Lee Guan. It's my track record against his. The choice is clear."[10] Indeed, the people I had given a good part of my life to for 10 years made their choice loud and clear.

I am glad that both Dr Poh and me fought a clean fight. Mr Lee had called me on my mobile phone at about 4.00 pm on the sixth day of campaign (Tuesday, 30 October). I was scheduled to hold a rally that night. I was then handing out flyers at a bus stop with my helpers. He was gentle in tone but firm in his voice. He asked if I was having a rally that night. I said "Yes". He then said he would like me to tell my voters that if they did not vote for me, Nee Soon East as an opposition-run constituency would become run-down. Instinctively, my reaction was that saying this may come across as a threat to my residents, that is "vote for me, or else!" Even though that would be "par for the course" in an election campaign, still I hesitated. I paused for about 15 seconds, took a deep breath and then replied, also in a firm voice, that I felt that there was no need to do that as I stood on my track record. I somehow felt it would be out of character for me to say something like that. My mind on this was quite clear. Not only would such a perceived threat not achieve its objective of securing more votes, it would be counterproductive and would undo some of the goodwill I had garnered with my residents. In the longer-run, it would negatively impact my standing with them. This time, it was Mr Lee's turn to pause. After about 10 seconds or so, he said, "Alright, you do it your way", or words to that effect. That night, then DPM Lee Hsien Loong came to speak at my rally where he included this reminder — of a rundown ward should they vote in an opposition MP — in his speech.

Mr Lee came by Nee Soon East on the eighth day of campaigning (Thursday, 1 November). He gave a brief press conference and then walked across the road to a neighbourhood mall to walk around some shops to greet residents and shake hands. Before he dropped by at Nee Soon East (that was already about 7.00 pm), he held a closed-door meeting with organisers of seven-month dinners from Nee Soon East, both from the temples and the more informal ones spread across the HDB blocks. That meeting lasted for about an hour and a half, and was held in a community centre in adjacent Chong Pang ward. Also present were MP K Shanmugam from Sembawang GRC and MP Ong Ah Heng from Nee Soon Central SMC. Their grassroots leaders had helped to contact the attendees to inform them of the meeting, some, I believe, only late that afternoon.

While Mr Lee had good intentions in meeting these seven-month dinner organisers, for which I am grateful, I had some misgivings as to how it was done. For one thing, I was not consulted and my views sought before the decision was made to proceed with the meeting. I knew that Ah Heng was helping to round up my seven-month dinner organisers, arising from a visit Mr Lee had made to Nee Soon Central (where Ah Heng was MP) the night before, to speak at a rally there. I think Mr Lee had expressed his concern about Nee Soon East to Ah Heng. The upshot is that the idea to hold such a meeting the following late afternoon or early evening was conceived. I was informed about the meeting early enough and was all geared up to be there. However, at about 2.00 pm to 3.00 pm that day, one of Mr Lee's security officers called me on my mobile phone to inform me that I need not attend the meeting. I was unhappy at being excluded, as I felt that I was on good terms with these seven-month dinner organisers. Even if there was any unhappiness on any matter, I felt that I would be able to explain my position, give any assurance to rectify the shortcomings, if necessary, and gain their renewed support. I felt that excluding me would send a wrong signal and undermine my position as their MP![11] Not only was the meeting not held in my own CC and contacting the attendees not done by my own grassroots leaders, now I would also not be present! In addition, I was told that just before the meeting started, an announcement was made that anyone from my grassroots in Nee Soon East should excuse himself or herself from the meeting. Though well-intentioned — probably to avoid any unpleasantness and to quickly get down to settle the crux of the unhappiness — I thought it was not necessary to do that.

I share all these sincerely now as learning points. Having gone through four GEs (contesting two of them and helping out at HQ for the other two uncontested GEs), I know full well that no one is immune from making mistakes in judgement and actions in the heat of battle over nine days of fierce campaigning. Without fail, there would be some "wrong turns" or missteps in every GE. Over nine days of campaigning, the situation would be fluid and decisions have to be made quickly. Still, I felt somewhat hard-done by at what had taken place over the last three to four days of campaigning in the 2001 GE.

Indeed, over the many GEs, there have been examples when well-intentioned interventions by the "big guns" from PAP HQ have been negative instead of positive, insofar as the local candidate is concerned. In my case, contrary to some media reports, I did not have the opportunity to tell Mr Lee not to "intervene" in my campaign the way he did.[12] That was in 2001 (still early days in terms of local candidate–PAP HQ interaction, where local candidates were not so bold or forthright), unlike the 2011 hustings, where Mr Sitoh Yipin famously asked HQ to keep out of the contest in Potong Pasir, which he then went on to win. However, as I shared earlier, I did tell Mr Lee that I could not take up his suggestion and say to my residents that their estate would become rundown should they vote in an opposition candidate.

I know that Mr Lee felt genuinely concerned about me, more so perhaps because I was an office-holder in the Law Ministry. However, was there a need for him to intervene the way he did? Perhaps not. For one thing, I was not personally attacked. While there were indeed some rumours circulating that, as a Christian, I did not support the temples and seven-month dinner groups, it was very clear to my residents who had seen me on the ground that this was not so. They had seen me at temples and seven-month dinners, shaking hands with all. That was why I chose to fight by just standing on my track record. Moreover, when informed of these rumours, I had already taken mitigating steps. My helpers arranged for me to visit one of the more prominent Chinese temples in Nee Soon East where I met the temple leaders, had tea with them and shook their hands. The Chinese media covered this visit prominently. In addition, incoming MP, Dr Ong Seh Hong, a grassroots leader of Nee Soon for 10 years, had spoken at my rally, sharing that I had attended all kinds of religious functions and festivals, including seven-month dinners. In all my years as MP, I had no problems with any of the religious groups in my constituency. Indeed, I had very warm ties with the leaders of the Nee Soon Combined Chinese temples, the Darul Makmur Mosque, the Star of the Sea Catholic Church and Evangel Family Church. I had meals with them and visited their premises occasionally. They actively supported my outreaches to the residents, chipping in with *ang pow* and food distribution, blood donation drives, free tuition classes and so on. Under the auspices of the Inter-Racial and Religious Confidence Circle, we held many activities and teas where we got to know each other well. Indeed, at the 2006 GE, a few key leaders of the Chinese temples in Nee Soon East spoke at my election rallies affirming their support for me. To be fair though, Mr Lee did not know the strength of my relationship with the religious leaders in Nee Soon East, including the Chinese temple and seven-month dinner organisers. Hence, understandably and true to his battle-hardened character, he reacted in the heat of battle the way he did.

As I had explained above, the wider context of the uncertainty surrounding a clear victory for me was that I was actually fighting a GRC team, with its "enhanced" resources. Moreover, I was fighting an election for the very first time and was doing so alone in a SMC. While the large majority of my residents were Hokkien-speaking, a dialect Dr Poh Lee Guan spoke fluently (by his admission, even better than his Mandarin), I did not speak Hokkien. Even though I spoke some Mandarin which, though improving, it was not of the colourful variety that would elicit loud cheers at election rallies. On the other hand, my opponent was a local boy who had links with the Chinese temples, through his father who sat on the committee of one of these temples.[13] The fact that I was a known, committed Christian made the contrast more telling. The media later (in an article published in 2005) said that one allegation then was that I "refuse(d) to attend any community function which featured a lion dance because of its non-Christian origins". Going on to refute it, the report continued, "(i)t's absurd because Prof Ho had clearly officiated at countless such events throughout his 14 years as MP."[14] The insidious nature of the problems that surfaced which dogged my campaign is perhaps best summarised by Mr Lee himself when he was reported to have said that there were "subterranean forces" at work!

So what was the root cause of the turbulence that erupted? Firstly, as mentioned earlier, a key grassroots leader of mine became a target through his perceived unethical business practices. This caused much angst and unhappiness to those who capitalised on the excitement of the GE to hit him. In the process, I was hit vicariously. Secondly, we innovated in our dealings with our constituency's seven-month dinner organisers. With the aim of making it easier for them to obtain their licences and permits to hold these dinners,[15] we had introduced a new system that year which enabled them to drop off their application forms anytime at my Community Centre, instead of having to come by my MPS only when it operated on Mondays. The CC staff would then hand the forms to me for my signature, after which the operators could collect them anytime from the CC. On paper, this was an improvement and made things easier for the organisers. Alas, all good intentions can go awry. As it transpired, the operators much preferred the old system that they were used to. Even though it required them to make a trip to my weekly MPS and constrained them to do so on only one night of the week,[16] they would rather do it than have the form deposited in the CC and not know the fate of their application until a few days or even a week or so later. The time lapse arose in some cases because I had not signed their forms immediately upon receiving them, either because I was overseas or was busy with work. There was a gap in the system that impeded its intended smooth functioning.

In addition, we introduced a new measure that was intended to facilitate the support of seven-month dinner organisers for the local community. Hence, just before the season of seven-month dinners started, we held a meeting of all the organisers at the Community Centre. The thinking was that this meeting would facilitate better communication as any problems or doubts could be cleared up on the spot. Such a meeting would also enable the organisers to know one another better. However, in our eagerness to get things done, the grassroots leader spearheading this tie-up apparently also asked the organisers whether they would be making any donations to the Citizens' Consultative Committee, to be channelled to worthy community causes. A piece of paper was passed around for anyone wishing to do so to indicate the amount. This move was again well-intentioned, but caused much unhappiness among those who attended the meeting. They saw it as pressurising them to donate something to the community. While they were happy to do so, and many indeed did so willingly over the years, to have to either write an amount down or pass it along, in front of all the others, was understandably just too much!

There is much to be learnt from this episode, especially in relation to dealing with different religious and community groups on the ground. For one thing, whenever anything new is introduced, communicating properly the rationale for it is important. Every effort should be made to explain why the old way of doing things is being changed. If this was done for these two new measures, we could have taken on board any useful feedback and adjusted the procedures accordingly. While efficiency is important, face, feelings and the personal touch were even more important. I do not recall my views being sought before these new procedures were introduced. Thus, the unhappiness surrounding their introduction only surfaced in the heat of the hustings, otherwise I would have dealt with them earlier! This is where Mr Lee's meeting with the seven-month dinner organisers probably had the positive impact of placating their hurt feelings. If he had not intervened, I suppose I could and should have held a media conference to put things right. However, these grounds of unhappiness were not made known to me then, and all this is conjecture now. This may have led some to think that I was not firm or decisive as a leader in the heat of battle![17] Admittedly though, notwithstanding my mental state which was affected by the turn of events, I should have put on a bolder front so that those doing battle alongside me would not be demoralised.

More importantly, I had not, but should have, anticipated the groundswell of unhappiness against the grassroots leader who was the target of the poison letter campaign. I should have nipped this problem in the bud much earlier and not have left it to boil over during the hustings. As this grassroots leader was very hardworking, had served in Nee Soon East for a long time and was sincere in serving the residents, I was blind to his business failings which had caused alarm bells to sound. Admittedly, this was a misjudgement on my part.

As shared earlier, in retrospect, the way the 2001 GE panned out ultimately led to my advantage. I continued to enjoy my stint as a strong Number 2 in MHA and MinLaw, and could gracefully retire from politics in 2011. For this, I have to thank then PM Goh for promoting me to Senior Minister of State and keeping me at MHA and MinLaw in 2001, and PM Lee Hsien Loong for letting me retire in 2011. Most of all, I am eternally grateful to Prof Jaya and Mr Wong Kan Seng for their timely intervention and critical input in getting me promoted in 2001.

Indeed, God works in mysterious ways!

Lessons in Leadership

1. As a leader, you must always be prepared to take tough and possibly unpopular measures such as asking a key staff, or indeed, your right-hand man to step down. You cannot be blind to faults that have surfaced. A compassionate and empathetic leader must balance these positive traits with a need to be realistic and practical and cut "losses" if the need arises. This could be a key helper, a pet project or an intended plan that runs up against strong opposition. This is where the axiom "better safe than sorry" applies.
2. There will be times when a leader will fail and fall badly. You must then pick yourself up. Assessments can go spectacularly wrong. Expectations, though well grounded, may fall far short. Anticipated accolades can turn into bruising brickbats. The thing to so is not to mope around or feel sorry for yourself, or worse, sink into depression. Get up, look ahead and get on with the job! This is where having a few mentors you can turn to or a support group of close friends will be useful.
3. In the heat of a crisis, a leader must remain calm and project a steady front. You must be a calming presence in the midst of anxiety and confusion. You must try to contain any self-doubts and be mindful that any negative sentiments may rub off on his team. How you come across — physically, emotionally, mentally — at this time is crucial. I learnt this the hard way — in the heat of battle. I was too transparent!
4. Be an authentic leader. Do not pretend to be what you are not. Hold on to your principles and beliefs. Be driven by values and these principles and beliefs in your actions. Ultimately, sincerity comes through. As you do so, while the core will remain unchanged, embedded in us, be prepared to reflect on whether these values, principles and beliefs may need some refinement, especially in their application.

Endnotes

1. Nee Soon East was one of nine single member constituencies (SMCs) in the 2001 GE. It was carved out of Sembawang GRC.
2. Even though I stayed till the end of my Meet the People sessions (MPS) to meet all who came to see me, after the 2001 campaign, I discovered that some residents were put off by having to wait a long time to see me. In fact, some left before doing so. They were frustrated at having to queue twice: the first time to be interviewed by my helpers and after that, to see me. Others were told by my helpers, good intentioned no doubt to save them the hassle of waiting to see me, that as theirs was a routine matter, there was really no need to see me. In both situations, the residents concerned ended up unhappy. I only found out about this after the 2001 GE and quickly changed the format of my MPS. In the new approach, we set up eight interviewing tables around a big room. I would then move around to meet and discuss each case as the interviewer processed the case with the resident.
3. Ah Heng was contesting Nee Soon Central SMC which was adjacent to Nee Soon East. He had won the seat in the 1996 GE, wrestling it back from the Singapore Democratic Party's Cheo Chai Chen. Cheo had defeated PAP's Ng Pock Too in the 1991 GE. While he was a newer MP than me, admittedly, he had more experience than me in fighting an election in a SMC. Before becoming an MP, Ah Heng was also active on the ground in other constituencies including Tanjong Pagar working alongside Mr Lee Kuan Yew.
4. *The Straits Times*, 30 October, p. H3.
5. As explained earlier, the Workers' Party had poured their resources originally intended for Aljunied GRC into Nee Soon East. At the three rallies held by them at Nee Soon East, their supporters living across the island converged on the field at block 440. The HDB carparks in the areas adjacent to the field were clogged with parked cars, some of which were parked illegally. It was no indication of electoral support for the Workers' Party candidate, Dr Poh Lee Guan, though.
6. *The Straits Times*, 31 October 2001, p. H1.
7. *The New Paper*, 3 November 2001, p. 8.
8. Just like in the recent 2015 GE, the bookies' odds were way off target!
9. *TODAY*, 5 November 2001, p. 3.
10. *TODAY*, 5 November 2001, p. 3.

11. This was indeed the case. After the GE, some residents who were unhappy with decisions of government agencies and who came to me to appeal, said that "they would complain to Mr Lee Kuan Yew" if their complaints were not satisfactorily resolved. The spectre of the GE hung over my head for a year or so after that!
12. This sets the record straight as *TODAY* (which Shin Min later carried on 18 May 2011) had reported that I had said "No" to Mr Lee coming to help me campaign in Nee Soon East in the 2001 GE
13. There were altogether six Chinese temples in Nee Soon East, located on three sites placed side by side.
14. *The New Paper*, 11 August 2005, p. 6.
15. These permits and licences had to be obtained from various agencies such as the Town Council, HDB, Police, etc. As grassroots advisor, I had to grant final approval.
16. On Mondays, when I held my MPS.
17. However, I must say that I was warmed by the many supportive emails, letters and cards that friends and acquaintances sent, with some offering to help me at short notice.

Chapter 7 | RETIRING FROM POLITICAL OFFICE

I was very fortunate to have had Ho Peng Kee with me in both ministries of Law and Home Affairs. I always found him a very steady and reliable colleague whom I could turn to assist me in tackling difficult issues in the ministries. In particular, he made valuable contributions in the effort to tackle the drug addiction problem, where he put in much effort working with many agencies. In the Ministry of Law, he made outstanding contributions promoting alternative dispute resolution.

Professor S Jayakumar, then Senior Minister,
in commenting on my retirement from politics

He is a very dependable and hard-working colleague whom I can completely trust in carrying out any assignment. Home Team officers will remember him as an approachable, big-hearted and principled person who championed policies that gave ex-offenders chances — the Yellow Ribbon Project and those involving volunteers in the rehabilitation process. He is an avid footballer and it will be apt for me to use a soccer analogy to describe him as a versatile player who excelled in all positions — whether it is to lead a wave of measures against loan sharks, to give a hard tackle to slow down drug abuse, or to play a nurturing role as a coach, such as growing the Home Team NS Association or grooming the younger civil servants...

Mr Wong Kan Seng, then DPM,
also in commenting on my retirement from politics

Home Team volunteers play an important part in ensuring Singapore's safety and security. You are ordinary Singaporeans, yet a special breed of people, who have and are making a quiet, yet extraordinary contribution to the Home Team in its various departments, individually and collectively... Now, with the HomeTeam Volunteers Network in place, our volunteers will be infused with a keener sense that they are really a part of a bigger HT family and derive a better understanding of the over-riding challenges facing the HT. Moreover, the network creates more opportunities for mutual interaction and learning among you and facilitates the implementation of best practices so as to level up.

Home Team Volunteers Day on 26 November 2011

For over 20 years, you have tirelessly served our NSE ward. With your hardworking, gentle, forgiving and kind approach, you have connected well with young and old alike. People from all walks of life have been able to reach out to you... Throughout these 20 years, you have not just been an MP but more importantly, you have become a close friend to us all.

Citizens' Consultative Committee Chairman Chris Lim on my retirement

Retiring from Political Office

General Elections were held on 3 May 2011. On 23 May, when the new Cabinet was sworn in, I left public office to resume life as an ordinary citizen. My feeling was one of gratitude and relief — grateful that I had the opportunity for 20 years to serve the cause of Singapore at the highest level and relieved that I had finished this part of my journey well.

By late 2009, I had decided that I would not stand for re-elections, and had informed PM of my decision. Not being a Cabinet Minister, I felt that it was open to me to ask not to be fielded. This would not be a problem as it would not weaken PM's core team. This is another reason why I am glad that I was not appointed a Cabinet Minister. I could leave politics gracefully and in a timely manner. Moreover, having devoted 18 years of my life to full-time politics, I felt it was time to enter the next phase or season of life. A key preoccupation of this next phase would be to be God's servant wherever He puts me.

The media reported that I had expressed my intention to do full-time missions work after retiring from politics. Actually, I did not say that. What I had shared with close friends and some church members was that I would like to be more involved in church and faith-based activities upon retirement from politics. This is quite different from going to the missionary field. Indeed, being more active in church and faith-based activities is one of the "balls" that I am juggling now, six years after retiring from politics.[1] The other two "balls" are lots of voluntary work and some part-time teaching.[2] So, there *is* life after politics!

My main voluntary work is chairing the Home Team Volunteer Network Steering Committee. The Ministry of Home Affairs has, in all, about 20,000 volunteers. Eight thousand of them are committed to specific responsibilities in the various Home Team departments. They include about 400 prominent Singaporeans in the various Councils and Committees such as the National Crime Prevention Council, National Fire Prevention and Emergency Preparedness Council, National Council Against

Drug Abuse, and Casino Regulatory Authority; 1,200 Voluntary Special Constabulary officers, 3,200 Prisons counsellors and befrienders, 700 Civil Defence Lion Hearters, 200 Crime Ambassadors and 350 Singapore Civil Defence Auxiliary Unit officers. Other key volunteers in the core group are those in the National Civil Defence Cadet Corps, National Police Cadet Corps, the Yellow Ribbon Project, Community Safety and Security Programme, and the Immigration and Checkpoints Authority Ambassadors. The other 12,000 volunteers comprise volunteers in key grassroots groups such as Citizens on Patrol and Neighbourhood Watch Groups/Zones, which are also affiliated to the People's Association.

Chairing this Committee is really an extension of what I had been doing for 18 years as office holder in MHA. During this time, I had interacted a lot with volunteers at functions and forums, making many friends in the process. Upon my retirement, then Permanent Secretary Benny Lim felt that the networks and friendships I had made should be tapped to foster a stronger sense of identity and *esprit de corps* in our MHA volunteers. Hence, with the blessings of then Home Affairs Minister, Mr K Shanmugam, the HTVN was launched.

Upon retiring, I continued to chair two committees at MinLaw; the first, to foster a stronger pro bono spirit in the legal fraternity; and the other, to steer the development of our Community Mediation Centres (CMCs). As in the case of the HTVN, MinLaw felt that my expertise in these areas, which I had been driving as office-holder in MinLaw for many years, should be tapped. I have since relinquished my chairmanship of the ProBono Committee. One other appointment (again on a voluntary basis) is that of being a member of the Board of Directors of the Singapore Mediation Centre. This platform of service, together with my being Patron of the Eagles Mediation and Conciliation Centre reflects a "going to the ground" approach, where I now serve in a hands-on capacity in areas where I had led reforms and initiatives at a higher national level whilst in office. This approach was a key reason why I agreed recently to be the Patron of RHT Rajan

Menon Foundation, a ground-level platform from which I believe I can provide leadership to the promising pro bono landscape developing among law firms in Singapore. Finally, I count it a privilege to have been recently appointed a Justice of the Peace (JP), an appointment I view with anticipation as there is no higher calling than to be a "peacemaker". Interestingly, compiling and processing the recommendations for JP appointments was one of my tasks at MHA over the years! Things have come full circle.

Other voluntary hats that have kept me busy are as Patron of the Children's Cancer Foundation, Adviser to Heartware Network, Adviser to the Football Association of Singapore and Adviser (previously Board member) to the Biblical Graduate School of Theology (BGST). These positions are in line with what I had said at the time of my retirement, which is that I would continue supporting worthy causes that promote sports, foster voluntarism, develop youth potential and engage in more faith-based work.

With much humility, I must say that my timing in politics has been perfect! As a committed Christian, I put it down to providential guidance. I entered full-time politics in 1993 after teaching at the Law Faculty, National University of Singapore for 14 years (1979–1993). Before that, I spent two good years solidifying my ground and honing my public image as a backbencher. Significantly, I took a few months' sabbatical leave from my teaching duties at the Law Faculty in 1992 to concentrate on my academic writing which tipped the balance and led to my promotion to Associate Professorship in early 1993. Shortly after that, in August 1993, I took long leave from the NUS, crossing over to the front bench to take up office as Parliamentary Secretary in the Ministry of Home Affairs and Ministry of Law. That is why, throughout the 18 years I was in politics, on leave from the NUS, friends, colleagues and residents alike called me "Prof", which to me is a term of endearment.

Looking further back, I believe that three somewhat unorthodox decisions earlier on had paved the way for me to enter politics many years later. The first was switching from the Science to Arts stream when I enrolled at the National Junior

College in 1971. In those days, the better students were automatically streamed into the Science stream at Secondary One level. Upon realising that my interests and strengths were in Arts subjects such as Literature and History, I made the switch after my 'O' level results. This way, I really enjoyed my two years as a "third-batch" NJC student (then the only junior college in Singapore and still a pioneer in junior college education). Here, I must credit NJC's founding Principal, Mr Lim Kim Woon (fondly called "Princi" by many of us), for instilling pro nation-building values in me. The second decision occurred in 1973, when my businessman father died within three to four months of being diagnosed with colorectal cancer, a few days short of his 50th birthday. I then switched from the study of business administration to law at the then Singapore University. Like all boys who were enrolled for NS in those days, we applied for and were allocated places at the local university a year or two before actual admission. My father's unexpected death released me from what I saw as my duty and responsibility as the older of two boys to prepare myself to take over his successful watch business; hence, the study of business administration. If I did not do law, I would probably not have entered politics. Lastly, in 1979, I was the only local graduate who had been accepted by a top law firm, Allen & Gledhill, for pupillage. I had already reported for "work" upon graduation (while waiting for the Practical Law Course, or PLC, to begin), when Prof Jaya, through then Sub-Dean Tan Lee Meng, sussed me out on returning to the Faculty of Law as a staff. I agonised for two weeks between two great options — staying on at Allen & Gledhill where I looked forward with keen anticipation to working with great pupil–masters and becoming a litigator, or becoming an academic with wonderful opportunities to interact with and influence young legal minds, and with a paid-for Masters in Law degree thrown in! I chose the latter, and that was how I ended up going to Harvard Law School on a Loke Foundation Scholarship. Looking back at these "twists and turns" in life, I am so thankful for the decisions that I took. I believe that, in its own way, each nudged me along towards the path of politics.

I left politics also at a good time. As is now clear to all, the 2011 GE was indeed a watershed election. In terms of electoral seats, the People's Action Party (PAP) lost six seats, including, for the first time, a Group Representation Constituency (GRC). Its winning margin, at 60.9%, dipped to the lowest ever. More importantly, as it became clear during the hustings, many Singaporeans expressed unhappiness with several government policies, especially those concerning housing, transport, and immigration. As local-born Singaporeans, they felt that the large influx of foreigners, including the thousands each year who take up permanent residence and citizenship, had made life less palatable and more unpleasant for them. Moreover, they felt that despite the very high Ministers' salaries, their problems on the ground were not adequately addressed. Worse, some felt that their views and unhappiness, articulated through various channels, were not seriously taken into account. The perception was that Ministers were more concerned about defending and justifying their actions and policies than genuinely listening to the grouses expressed, reflecting on them carefully and then addressing them sincerely. Even if these grouses could not be fully addressed, the process would have had a positive effect on these disgruntled citizens, many of whom later voted from their hearts to send a signal to the ruling party.

The 2011 GE results and its aftermath, especially the impact on the social compact between the government and people, are well-documented and fully canvassed in the media. There have been several key consequences. One fall out is that Ministers' salaries were significantly reduced. Another is that all politicians, both ruling and opposition, became more active online. On this, I must say quite candidly that this was perfect timing for me. Unlike most politicians today, I did not blog or maintain a Facebook account. Even though I accepted the fact that online engagement was an inexorable tide that could not be resisted, as I was phasing out of politics, I kept a low profile, preferring to press on with the personal, face-to-face approach. At most, when residents sent me requests and complaints by email, I would deal with these and reply them online. A third consequence was that Ministers and MPs began to walk the ground more frequently, more informally, and sometimes unannounced and with no fanfare. I applaud this move. This is something I had done when in office, both in and outside of Nee Soon East. Thus, popping in at nearby Newton hawker centre in shorts to have a meal with or *da bao* (to pack) a meal for my family, enjoying a jog at the Botanical Gardens in the evening on my own with no fanfare, cycling around Nee Soon East with key grassroots leaders or going on work-related walkabouts was part of my routine. I found these occasions liberating, making life as an office-holder less constraining and more like what fellow Singaporeans experience too.

What do I mean by "work-related walkabouts"? Early on in my time in MHA, I had visited a few discos to assess the situation there, from the law and order and drug abuse angles. A small team of MHA officers walked with me and we went about our business quietly and discreetly, with no media coverage or security officers gently moving bystanders aside. On another occasion, the weekend before I responded to several parliamentary questions on vice in Singapore, I quietly drove around the Geylang *lorongs* late at night to assess the situation myself. And on many occasions, while driving around Singapore on a Sunday, I would be surveying the vacant plots of state land and thinking of "fun" ways to use them.

I notice that Ministers and MPs these days are less formal and make an effort to interact with the crowd when they grace functions. They walk in without much fanfare and speak with less pomp and ceremony, often taking the microphone in their hands and, sometimes, speaking without a rostrum. Other than making points from the prepared script, they *ad lib* more, feeling the mood of the crowd as they make their impromptu remarks. This has helped them to connect more effectively with the audience. Those who have heard me speak at functions will find this approach familiar. I had espoused and adopted this informal way all along. In fact, quite often, when I mingled with the audience after the formal ceremony was over, many would remark to me that my impromptu remarks resonated with them more.

In Parliament, there is much more impromptu and *ad hoc* debate nowadays, less reading from a prepared script. That is good and is what it should be. After all, the Hansard calls the proceedings "parliamentary debates"! Those who follow parliamentary debates closely will know that, in my time, I "debated" more than "read" while on my feet in Parliament. Indeed, in my maiden speech in Parliament (*see* Annex A), I was already engaging in "on-the-feet" spontaneous debate with Opposition MPs Chiam See Tong and Ling How Doong.

When I read from a prepared speech in Parliament, for example, in taking a Bill through in its first reading, or when reading out a main reply to a parliamentary question, I tried to do so with some passion and in an engaging — not a dull or deadpan — tone. Very often, my replies, especially those emanating from MHA, would elicit further questions from Members. My preparation would then come into play. I would have a good debate with MPs, both from the ruling and opposition parties and whether elected, nominated or non-constituency! Each time, my thick black clip folder would be full of yellow tabs sticking out, marking the pages setting out the issues which I expected MPs to raise. Following the 2011 GE, with more elected opposition members in Parliament, the debates became more intense and interactive.

Moreover, the speeches, both from the front bench as well as backbench, and both from ruling party members as well as opposition parties' members, have a more distinct political edge and overtone. Not unexpectedly, there is now in everything that MPs do an eye to the next General Elections! Before the 2011 watershed General Elections, I would say that debates in parliament were 90% governance-focused and only 10% politics-focused. Post-2011, the equation became about 75%–25%. Now, it has settled at about 80%–20%. The Singaporean electorate is a matured one and would like to see more light than heat in Parliamentary debates. To me, this is still an acceptable split, and not a bad outcome for Singapore as long as policies get refined and improved as a result of these debates. However, I dread the day when, as is the case in some countries, the energy in parliamentary debates are dissipated into winning arguments for argument sake; or worse, slamming your opponents' points just to appear good! There is little focus on debating policies to achieve good governance. Rather, the focus is on gaining the upper hand politically. More heat than light will then be generated.

Six years now into life as a private citizen, I am enjoying my freedom from the public glare more and more each day. I walk around the shopping malls and jog around our parks incognito. Now and then, someone may recognise me and smile or wave. What gives me much joy is when someone stops to chat and tells me that he or she lives in Nee Soon East or had previously lived there. Then we would chat for a while about "old times"! Over this time, while most Singaporeans who recognise me remain warm, I can sense the special warmth of these NSE residents and ex-residents. It is as though our shared memories over the years are stored neatly just beneath the surface and are pushed up into our consciousness, melting away the years when a familiar face appears.

In my season in politics, working with so many good-hearted Singaporeans from all walks of life, I hope I have helped to make Singapore a better place. I had entered politics in 1991 in response to then PM Goh's call to build a kinder, gentler Singapore. In 2017, Singapore has indeed become a kinder, gentler place and a more open, dynamic society. While Singapore has definitely become more crowded and cosmopolitan, and our society has become more complex, my view is that on the whole, Singaporeans are more compassionate and courteous and more aware of the need to keep united. Singapore society has indeed matured. On making Singapore a better place, I remain eternally grateful for the many opportunities to shape policies that helped less fortunate Singaporeans. Some were pioneering efforts which others have, since their introduction and early development, built upon. At a personal level, over the years, I had interacted with a wide diversity of people, from MPs (both PAP and opposition as well as NMPS), to civil servants from across the Ministries, to grassroots leaders and volunteers in all shapes, sizes and backgrounds, to Ministers and their officials from other countries, to my very own community leaders and residents. I thank God for each and everyone of them.

I am also humbled by the many opportunities that came my way to mentor and help nurture some of the younger Members of Parliament and political office-holders. They include my successors in some of the appointments I held, including Gan Kim Yong (PAP Community Foundation Executive Committee Chairman), Zainudin Nordin (FAS President), Teo Ho Pin (Sembawang Town Council and Community Development Council Chairman), Masagos Zulkifli (Minister of State, MHA) and Patrick Tay (MP for Nee Soon East, now part of Nee Soon GRC).[3] I daresay that in each of these positions, I handed to my successor a strong ship. This is a philosophy of leadership which I hold, which is that you should leave when "the going is good". This way, your successor need not spend time and expend energy cleaning up any mess, but can concentrate on building on the strong foundations and work you leave behind. Also, help your successor settle in, and hope and pray that he does a better job than you to make things even better. On this, I am glad that Patrick Tay had continued to look after Nee Soon East very well after he took over from me in May 2011.[4] He had understudied me for about two to three months before the General Elections. During this time, I took the opportunity to introduce him to the residents. With him standing next to me, I light-heartedly told them that he would make a better leader than me. After all, he was "taller, more handsome, sang and spoke Mandarin better than me and knew how to speak Hokkien as well." Most importantly, he bore the key characteristic of all MPs looking after Nee Soon East, that is, like my predecessor, Charles Chong and me, he had a ready smile. These remarks often drew chuckles from those present. In the two Ministries, I had the great privilege of working with many successive cohorts of good, and some outstanding, civil servants at both MHA and MinLaw. Topping the list would be Benny Lim (as Permanent Secretary, MHA); Lau Wah Ming (as Deputy Secretary, MinLaw) and SCDF Commissioner James Tan (as Vice-President, Home Team NS Association).

In turn, I had learnt from many older politicians including several DPMs whom I had worked closely with. Dr Tony Tan was Minister in charge of Sembawang GRC when I was a rookie MP in 1991. In my second term as MP (1996–2001), I was his right-hand man in running the Town Council and Community Development Council. Dr Tan struck me as a man who knew exactly what he wanted. He was a master of the areas of work he handled, for example, in running the various Ministries and other portfolios he was in charge of over his long tenure in office as well as in winning over Sembawang constituents on the ground. A key strength of Dr Tan's was getting things done efficiently, that is, deriving maximum results with just the right amount of effort. Prof Jaya was a real gentleman and treated with due consideration everyone he worked with. He was gentle but firm. Almost a fatherly figure, he gave those he worked with the warm assurance that their views mattered and would be taken into account. I have always felt that his somewhat serious-looking demeanour did him a great disservice as he is clearly a warm-hearted, caring man, and with a sense of humour too! Mr Wong's strength is his decisiveness in making decisions and tenacity in getting things done. MHA officers knew that he would back them up. He and I worked well together, my compassionate disposition complementing his tough demeanour. He was a great Minister of Home Affairs for Singapore, although his style may have put some people off. Current DPM Teo Chee Hean, whom I worked with at PCF for about 10 years, had a good mix of all these qualities and was, on most accounts, a popular politician.

Looking back on my 62 years, as a committed Christian, what is clear is that God had guided me through various phases of life, with each phase's experiences helping to prepare me for the later phases that followed. In *Junior College Education in Singapore* published by the Ministry of Education in the mid-1990s to help 'O' level students choose the JCs to apply to, I shared that "we walk life's journey a step at a time. No one can know for sure what lies ahead. However, at each phase of life, we strive to do our best — serving, giving, receiving and growing in the process. Each phase helps to build us up for the next phase. I will always cherish my JC days..." As an office-holder in the Singapore University Student Law Society and chairman of the 1976 Dinner and Dance Organising Committee, I wrote in the programme, "...varsity life does not comprise only of academic fulfillment. The full potentiality of exposure to human experiences is always there — latent — waiting to be tapped... The key is in your hand. Use it... If after four years in Law School, you cannot honestly recount the pleasurable moments shared with friends and lecturers, then you have yourself to blame."

Leadership training began at an early age for me. Born into a family of eight children, and growing up with seven (my third sister died of cancer in 1957 when she was eight years old; I was then three years old), with four older sisters "taking care"of me, I had learnt to be sensitive and gentle from young. As a very active student in ACS, NJC and the Singapore University, fully immersed in sports, drama, debates and student leadership, I picked up valuable social and leadership skills. Indeed, surrounded by so many older sisters, I think sports played a key part in preventing me from becoming effeminate! At many public forums while in office, I had shared that active involvement in many extra curricular activities (ECAs) through the years had honed my leadership and relational skills. As shared earlier in Chapter 5, I had played many sports competitively since young. In particular, I have played competitive football in some six to seven teams (from when I was 13 years old in secondary one to the time when I was an Officer Cadet School trainee during my NS days) and had captained most of them. Acting and debating were something that shaped me considerably. At NJC, in 1971, I won the Best Actor award in my portrayal of an elderly father of three girls in *The Barretts of Wimpole Street* (one of my three "daughters" was Ms Jane Ittogi, who later married DPM Tharman Shanmugaratnam). As JC1 students, we had great fun rehearsing together! As a first-year law faculty student at the Singapore University in 1975, I anchored the University debating team as final speaker in a nationally-televised inter-tertiary institutions debate. I share all this with great humility, thankful for the many opportunities that my growing up years had thrown up. It is also a testimony and, hopefully, an encouragement to young readers that life is not only about doing well in examinations.

As a national serviceman and NS officer, I learnt to interact with and lead men who came from diverse backgrounds. A newly-commissioned second lieutenant in the SAF, and all of 20 years old, I found myself as a finalist in the Outstanding Young Singaporean Awards in 1974. Pitted against older and more established Singaporeans, including former Senior Minister of State in the Ministry of Foreign Affairs, Zainul Abidin Rasheed, I did not win. Winners in other years have included TT Durai (1972), Prime Minister Lee Hsien Loong (1975) and Minister for Foreign Affairs, Dr Vivian Balakrishnan (1985). My wide interactions with people extended to the time when I was a university don as I did not follow the usual path of an academic immersed in teaching and academic writing. Indeed, some of my friends considered me "quite mad" as I was interacting with students all of my waking hours. At the Law Faculty, NUS, I was Sub-Dean and then Vice-Dean (1987–1992), where my responsibilities included overseeing student activities and welfare. As Resident Fellow and then Master of Kent Ridge Hall (1981–1993), I lived and interacted with many very active undergraduates from the different faculties, where my life was lived almost like an "open book"! Indeed, with no prior experience in party politics or grassroots work, my experiences at the Law Faculty and Kent Ridge Hall stood me in very good stead when I became MP in 1991. Other than being the youngest Hall Master (35 years old in 1988)[5] at that time, I was also a relatively young church elder (34 years old in 1987).[6]

Providentially, God had prepared me for the key areas I worked on at MHA and MinLaw. My interest in Alternative Dispute Resolution (ADR) was stirred when I wrote my LL.M. paper at Harvard Law School on the Singapore Arbitration Act. Later on, I contributed the Singapore chapter to the publication *Arbitration Laws of the World*, published by the International Chamber of Commerce. My involvement on the Management

Committee of one of the first halfway houses in Singapore — the House of Hope — in the late 1980s gave me valuable insights on how to tackle the drug scourge at MHA. My active involvement in sports all through school and university marked me out as a sportsman who knew the issues well as COSS Deputy Chairman and FAS President. All my years of working with young people in the Law Faculty, Kent Ridge(KR) Hall of Residence and as Chairman of the National Police Cadet Corps Council (1988–1993) helped me to better understand them as Chairman of the Inter-Ministry Committee Against Juvenile Delinquency (IMJD). Such preparation went as far back as kindergarten, when I spent two wonderful years at Kum Yan Kindergarten which grounded me strongly in my love for Chinese. This grounding helped me to secure a 'B3' grade for my 'O' levels examination for second language in 1970, as a student of ACS, quite unheard of in those days! Hence, recovering my oral Mandarin skills was relatively quick when I became an MP.

Not only in terms of experience did earlier phases prepare me for my contribution in the latter phases, God also brought many people into my life throughout these phases. Some, I have helped to shape; others have helped shape me into what I am today. Some, I have shown love to; others have shown love to me. Publicly, I have said many times that Singapore is like a big family. Our lives cross all the time. You meet in a later phase of life people you had met in an earlier phase in a different capacity, wearing a different hat. How warm they feel towards you is influenced in part by the quality of the interaction in the earlier encounter; in particular, how you have treated them. I have experienced this many times during the different phases of life I have been through, including the current phase where I have retired from politics. I am happy to say that many friends I got to know when in school or university have remained friends for life.[7] Even though we have not kept in close touch, these are friends with whom you connect easily once contact is re-established. You never know when you need your friends. This thought has helped to keep me humble throughout my time in politics.[8]

It was in this spirit that a former law student and my "block head" at Block C, Kent Ridge Hall, N Sreenivasan or "Cheenu" (as he was fondly called), made an appointment to see me at MinLaw in 1994 to seek support for the Law Society's Law Awareness Week. Cheenu was the organising chairman of this biennial event, where lawyers gave talks and conducted free clinics for needy Singaporeans over a weekend at a venue normally located in the heartlands, such as Woodlands or Ang Mo Kio. I was happy that he approached me without any inhibition. To me, this meant that our time together in the Hall was so meaningful, the comfort level created high enough for him to do so. There were many such occasions when time evaporated whenever I met "people from the past"! I put Cheenu in touch with various agencies that provided financial and logistical support. After that initial approach, I continued to do my part to assist subsequent annual Law Awareness Week events. For this, the Law Society gave me an award for supporting pro bono efforts after I retired from politics.

In the same way, I have met several present and past Nee Soon East residents recently in my capacity as Justice of the Peace. I have had the privilege of solemnising their marriages — what a joy it is! I also meet many of my former law students and KR hall residents at various functions. Many of them are now accomplished lawyers, judges, performing artistes, professionals, businessman and such. We chat easily on these occasions, buoyed sometimes by the fact that I still remember their names, at least in part, if not in whole!

Another common strand that has emerged is that in some of the key areas I was involved in, I had, in one way or another, helped to lay the ground work upon which later policies were built on. These areas include helping foreign domestic workers settle down better here, getting more Singaporeans to exercise and bond through brisk walking clubs, promoting cycling as a form of leisure or means of transport, garnering community support in keeping Singapore safe and secure, fighting the scourge of loansharking, reaching out to prisoners' families while their breadwinner is incarcerated, more effective rehabilitation for inmates who are mentally-handicapped and enhancing professionalism in our PCF kindergartens, including reaching out to young ones with special needs.

Will I leave the public/community service arena totally? I hope not. Serving your fellow men, in one form or another, should be life-long. However, one thing is certain; I will continue to live each day to the fullest. As I did for 20 years in public office, going forward, I will endeavour to discharge my responsibilities, whether public or private, to the best of ability. My philosophy remains the same, that is, to look out for and grasp the opportunities as they present themselves. As a committed Christian, I seek God's will and guidance for this last phase of my "working" life. He has guided me through so many exciting milestones in my life. I continue to trust in Him, that He knows what is best for me.

The lessons in leadership never ends. Each phase of life builds on the previous ones. In this way, we are never done until our last breath. And even then, if we have lived our life well, we leave a lasting legacy that continues in the lives of those whom we had interacted with and who take up the mantle after us. As Søren Kierkegaard[9] so poignantly reminds us, "Life can only be understood backward, but it must be lived forward." So *carpe diem*, seize the day!

As I end this sharing of my political journey, I return to where I had started — Nee Soon East, my home for 20 years. In the words of my Community Centre Management Committee (CCMC) chairman K Gopal, it has been a "Journey of Passion"! (*see* Appendix D).

Lessons in Leadership

1. Always think about and work on succession planning. Who is the best person to take over from you (if the choice is yours)? How do you groom him (or her)? If the choice is not yours, work with the person chosen to prepare him to take over. Leave him a strong ship, stronger than the one you inherited. Do not undermine him by highlighting your own achievements in glowing terms. Give him the latitude to chart his own course, while building on your legacy. Expect that he will do better than you, so that the organisation you have invested time and effort in will become better and stronger! A corollary to all this will be to know when to step down.

2. Whatever you do in life, no matter how high or how low your station in life, remain humble. Be yourself. Do not put on airs. Be quietly confident that whatever you are doing, you are doing something that helps Singapore become a better place. In our different phases of life, our paths will intersect with many people. At different points in time, we will interact with them in different capacities; sometimes, they will need your help and at other times, you will need theirs. Say, if you put someone down or treat someone harshly because you are "up there", later on in life, that person may become your "boss", benefactor (gives you a job offer or directorship in a company) or your child's teacher or even father- or mother-in-law! When we pass on from this world, a good part of our legacy will be how others remember us, based on our interactions with them. For some, it will be how our words and actions have impacted their lives, hopefully positively!

3. Observe, interact and learn from those who are more experienced than us. Strive to grow in every way — professionally, intellectually, emotionally, mentally, socially and spiritually. All of us should have mentors we can learn from in the different areas of our life. They need not be formally installed or acknowledged as such. As we interact with them, observe them. In this way, we grow. Think about why they do things in a certain way. In turn, we become mentors to younger ones in our own time. Then, we must be prepared to spend time to pass on lessons learnt in life.

Endnotes

1. I have returned to church leadership as an elder in the church session. Other than that, I am also more active taking on more teaching and pastoral responsibilities. I went on my first mission trip — a five-day medical mission to a remote village in Cambodia in December 2011. It was a heartwarming and eye-opening experience, where I relived my national service days living in simple and rough conditions, but very good for the soul!
2. I have re-joined the Law Faculty, NUS on a part-time basis as an Associate Professorial Fellow. In addition to conducting some guest lectures and advising on various matters, such as pro bono activities at the NUS, I have also shared on "Good Governance in Singapore" at various fora including the Nanyang Technological University's Executive Development Programme, the Management Development of Singapore (MDIS), the Eagles Communications, the Police Cooperative Society, etc., to diverse groups of foreign participants.
3. Patrick has since been deployed to West Coast GRC looking after the Boon Lay ward.
4. Louis Ng is now the MP looking after the Nee Soon East ward.
5. Other Hall Masters like Professor Wong Wai Chow, Professor Tan Lee Meng and Professor Lawrence Chia were considerably older than me.
6. I was elected and served as church elder in the session of Mount Carmel Bible Presbyterian Church, providentially for three years just before I became an MP. When I entered politics, I did not stand for elections to the church session as I wanted to keep separate these two "public" offices. In line with my church practice and tradition, I remained an elder (which is for life) but chose to be involved only in private ministry areas such as the church prayer meeting and personal counselling.
7. My Singapore University Law Faculty class, in 2015, celebrated "40 Years of Friendship" marking the time since we were raw freshmen in 1975! Those who came enjoyed a great evening of fun and nostalgia.
8. For example, a person whom I have kept in touch with through my season in politics is someone I will call "V". V hails from the Raffles Institution. He was two years my junior in Law School but encountered personal problems while in his second year and did not

complete his studies. I got to know him briefly as fellow students. When I became a public figure, he contacted me for help. Other than connecting him to his MP at that time, I have continued to help him with a small *ang pow* three or four times a year to help him tide through his difficulty. In 1998, he sent me a note with a touching tribute as follows:

In a hostile world
where I struggle to find a living
In a season fast drying
a friend remembers
another and gives
out of his kind heart.
Illness is debilitating
But Jehovah Jireh provides
through friends,
manna for the day
light to show the way.
He sits in the council of elders
In parliament
and though silver and gold I have none
I thank God in a simple prayer
for a kind and generous friend
in Peng Kee

9. He was a Danish philosopher and theologian who lived in the earlier part of the 19th century.

Appendix A	**MY MAIDEN SPEECH IN PARLIAMENT**

Mr Ho Peng Kee (Sembawang GRC): Mr Speaker, Sir, I rise in support of the motion standing in the name of the Member for Hong Kah GRC.

The Next Lap is a well-considered and finely-crafted document. I urge every Singaporean to read it. Its 160 pages hold forth a vision for a nation and capture the aspirations of a people. The Member for Hougang asked for the Government's response to the elections. Well, the answer to me is clear. It is to fulfil its promise to level up society by implementing the Next Lap. The vision spans 20 to 30 years, a time frame which some Singaporeans cannot grasp. Shorter-term objectives are required and these the Next Lap provides, for threading through the vision are shorter-term objectives and strategies.

In addition, the President in his Address has continued the process of unveiling programmes which translate these objectives into reality. Vision, objectives and strategies, and programmes — indeed a laudable approach, and I may add, a serious approach. The programmes are carefully thought out and they are certainly not jokes. They may not be perfect, but they are not jokes. This morning, we hear the Member for Bukit Gombak describing many of these programmes as jokes. I think this cannot be so. For if indeed they are jokes, then I am afraid more than two million Singaporeans have become the butt of jokes. I say this typecasting by the Member for Bukit Gombak is itself a poor, frivolous, joke cracked in bad taste.

Sir, we should be mindful that Singaporeans respond to the Next Lap differently. Some, like me, find the vision inspiring, others find it bewildering. Some look forward eagerly to the Next Lap. Others are more wary. They fear that they cannot adjust. I hope this will be borne in mind as specific programmes are further firmed up and shared with the public. As we level upwards, we should be mindful that Singaporeans have different levels of capacity to enjoy the good life. Also, in our pursuit of market-oriented pragmatic policies, we should be prepared to exercise flexibility and compassion in enforcing the rules against genuine hardship cases, for indeed, genuine hardship cases there will always be. On these premises, Sir, I firmly believe that there is a place under the sun in Singapore for everyone.

Sir, many speakers have spoken on the substantive matters raised in the President's Address. As the penultimate speaker of the new MPs to speak, I wish to return to the big picture and focus on an important underlying theme — that Singaporeans should stay united and pull together to accomplish the tasks ahead. Indeed, I think pulling together is a very apt description. For, indeed, building a country is not unlike tugging in a tug-of-war. The attributes are common. You need strength, you need stamina, you need perseverance, you need timing, you need technique. You need to place your people along the rope correctly, in the right positions. I think, in this regard, I am sure all of us will agree with the Member for Hougang, that Singaporeans, as a people, are also important in that they are pulling together with the Government. I do not think any of us wants to downgrade the contribution of Singaporeans in this process. And you need a good anchorman in a tug-of-war, not unlike the goalkeeper in football, and finally, you need balance.

I wish to examine three areas where I feel balance is important to achieve greater unity. Sir, my first area of concern is this. I sincerely feel that Singaporeans should be more affirming all round, people towards people, people towards Government, Government towards people.

What do I mean by being affirming? Singaporeans should seek to bring out the best in each other. As we share a common destiny, we also have common accountability and responsibility, one to the other. One expression of mutual affirmation is in our approach towards voicing complaints or criticism, whether against national policies, Government departments or indeed against each other.

Some may say that Singaporeans complain rather freely, sometimes negatively. How then may one complain positively? I offer three suggestions. First, balance complaints with compliments. Nothing, and no one is totally bad, not our society, not Singaporeans and certainly not our Government. For sure, it is not right all the time, but neither is it wrong all the time. In fact, I am sure Singaporeans will agree when I say that our Government is right most of the time. It must be so. Otherwise we will not be where we are today, a nation standing proud in a community of nations with a standard of living that has indisputably increased over the years, despite what the Member for Potong Pasir may say, where citizens have a sense of self-worth and respect — and I think that is important — and who are involved in the shaping of the nation's destiny.

On this point, I know that Mr Chiam's assertion has been decisively rebutted by Members, but let me just add my small contribution. Let us not take an episodic approach. Let us not draw a trend by referring to isolated instances or episodes or professions.

Mr Chiam See Tong (Potong Pasir): Have you been in an Opposition camp?

Mr Ho Peng Kee: Sir, I guess I must get used to interruptions by the Member for Potong Pasir.

Returning to my point on complaints, I urge Singaporeans to maintain a balance when they criticise the Government. After all, the Government is composed of individuals. They, like us, need affirmation. Let us not take for granted our political leaders. Like teachers, I hope Singaporeans will continue to hold our political leaders in high regard. But please do not get me wrong. I am not saying that we must always agree with the Government. What I am saying is that, even if Singaporeans are quick to criticise policies they disagree with, they should be as fearless to speak out for policies they agree with. That is the first point.

Secondly, I feel there is an art to complaining. Complaints should not demoralise. No doubt, they should have a chastening effect but the overall impact should be one that builds up. A good feeling is generated that the system has become a better one without personal feelings being unnecessarily hurt. Words should be chosen wisely and one should not over-state one's case.

Thirdly, if we are complaining against an existing practice or situation, we should consider the alternatives as part of the process of thinking through. We should put ourselves in the position of the other party and empathise with his concerns. May I suggest that both Mr Cheo, the Member for Nee Soon Central, and Mr Low, the Member for Hougang, and this morning, in fact, the Member for Bukit Gombak, also raised the same point, look dispassionately at the reasons given by HDB as to why MPs cannot have offices at subsidised rates in void decks. I am sure that Singaporeans will agree that in order to maximise precious space, there is a need to prioritise use, and that social and community needs should rightly have precedence over political ones.

In any case, Opposition Members are not the only ones who are unhappy. PAP MPs have to make adjustments too. On this point, Mr Ling talked about a contract being formed between him and the Government. Yes, I think any first year law student will know that the acceptance of an offer may lead to a contract. But, in any case, without going into the nitty-gritty as to whether indeed there is a contract between him and the Government, I think all of us also know, even as laymen, that before one enters into a contract, one must examine the fine print carefully before signing on the dotted line. I am afraid Mr Ling has not done this or, worse still, he has misread the fine print.

In complaining or criticising, I say let us maintain a balance. The complainant should not only focus on his rights, but also on his duties as well. At the same time, he should also appreciate the rights of the other party. In one clear instance, as consumers, Singaporeans should be prepared to complain when aggrieved. There are retailers in Singapore who deal unfairly with consumers. Whether Singaporeans or tourists, this is unacceptable in a Singapore that prides itself as a shopping paradise. In this regard, echoing the call of the Consumers' Association of Singapore,

I urge the Government to set up an office with some of the functions of the Office of Fair Trading in the United Kingdom to deal with such errant retailers. Here, I declare my interest as Vice President of CASE.

The second area where we should continue to maintain a balance is in our drive to discover our cultural roots. I agree with the present approach of tapping strengths that lie in our rich cultural diversity. Unlike the Member for Potong Pasir, I do not think that this approach would lead to racial segregation or, worse still, discord. Each cultural heritage has something to offer. It serves as an anchor to that community in the midst of a rapidly changing world. In our quest for a Singaporean identity, it is correct that we do not dilute these distinctives and settle for a weak vanilla flavour. Our various cultures are like tributaries originating from the sources of different great rivers, all converging in a lake, each bringing with it rich harvests of marine life, peculiar to that source, a rich diversity, but one lake. When cross-fertilisation of the life forms occurs — these life forms in our analogy would represent cultural attributes — well, new forms of marine life emerge which are of a higher order, stronger, more hardy, that is a bonus. Before this happens, each marine life in itself is a rich addition to life in the lake, which is home to all. In the meantime, the lake, like Singapore, will develop its own distinctives because of its geographic location, because of the quality of its water and so on.

However, as we know, discovering one's roots is only one process. Two other processes are involved. One is that Singaporeans are also encouraged to discover each other's heritage, and I think that is important. For knowledge of each other's cultural heritage would lead to yet a third process, an appreciation of the commonalities such as the common values or possible overlapping historical origins of the various cultures. Knowledge leads to understanding, understanding to appreciation, appreciation to harmony.

Let us keep the three processes in balance, as we continue our present steady course towards achieving a Singaporean identity.

I guess, as we go along this process, there is a need to continually focus on these three processes.

But here, may I suggest, that more be done to promote better understanding and wider practice of our Shared Values. Secondly, more should also be done to promote greater awareness of how Singaporean pioneers have contributed to the building up of early Singapore. Thirdly, I would like to suggest that highlight be given to our Singaporean distinctives, such as our food, our lifestyle, our colloquial expressions, our pastimes, our leisure pursuits, traditional games and so on.

My third area, Sir, is this. I would like to see greater efforts in promoting community life in Singapore. Community life straddles many forms and facets of living in Singapore. It is called for in settings, such as the family, work place, tertiary institutions, in schools, professional or social interest groups, neighbourhoods and so on. Community life requires adjustment and accommodation. Excessive individualism and individualistic behaviour are incompatible with cohesive community life. The President warns against this in his Address. Singaporeans by all means should develop individuality from which creativity springs. After all, everyone is unique. But the rich diversity that nurturing individuality engenders should be balanced with the accommodation of group interests that community life requires. In this context, I support the recent ban on chewing gum. Here, group interests, such as the safety and convenience of MRT commuters, protection of the environment and costs, should rightly prevail. Having failed to educate the public for so many years, the Government has imposed this ban as a means of last resort. Having said this, Sir, please permit me to make two points, perhaps for the benefit of future exercises of like nature.

My first point is this. I feel the ban would have gone down better with the public if notice had been given that the Government was contemplating the ban. The message would then be this: We will ban unless the situation improves and stays improved. This, in my view, would serve two purposes. First, to give the culprits what in law is called a *locus poenitentiae* or an opportunity to repent. The second purpose and I think, more importantly, to give Singaporeans as a whole, particularly gum chewers who dispose their gum in the proper way, as well as parents, teachers and friends of the recalcitrant chewers, the opportunity to exercise group and peer pressure. I feel that this will enhance people bonding as the concept of mutual accountability and responsibility will be reinforced. Also, it will enhance bonding between Government and people.

My second point on the ban is this: perhaps a short grace period could have been considered for traders to dispose of their stocks. The money involved in each case may not be much, but still it is the thought that counts.

Sir, to summarise this third area of concern I say this. Let us continue to open up and be warm to each other as fellow Singaporeans, whether it be in the case of Singaporeans travelling, living or working abroad, or right here in Singapore, in our offices, schools, hostels, karaoke lounges, messes, indeed in public places. Let us sing our National Anthem and our community and national songs with greater gusto, and not just during National Day celebrations. Another area, let us challenge and encourage one another to keep fit. Here Mr Ling has brought up the point about kidney patients who, he would have us believe, are a neglected group. This is definitely not true. The Member for Cheng San GRC has very firmly rebutted the point. But in addition, all of us will applaud the good work of the NKF. Incidentally, the President of the NKF is, I believe, the Senior Minister of State for Education and the Patron is, I believe, the President himself. In addition to the points that the Member for Cheng San GRC raised, the Government also introduced legislation recently where kidney organs are now "in" unless one "opts out". So, I certainly cannot say that kidney patients are a neglected lot.

In summary, Sir, I urge fellow Singaporeans to maintain a sense of balance and perspective in all that we do. Much has been achieved but more can be achieved. The enduring underlying challenge for Singaporeans is to stay united and to pull together.

Let us do this not only for ourselves but for our children and our children's children.

Before I close, may I take this opportunity to respond to a point raised by the Member for Potong Pasir. He says that the Government should loosen its grip on the universities and grant it more autonomy. He claims that the Government has put the universities on a leash, and would have us believe that there is fear on the campuses. I think this allegation is unfair and certainly untrue. Moreover, it is sweeping. Like Dr Michael Lim, I feel it deserves a rejoinder.

Let me assure him that all is well with our universities. We are not perfect, but neither are we the stifling and mindless institutions that Mr Chiam would have us believe them to be. I am sure both my NUS colleagues and NTU staff, many of whom are engaged in important research, will take issue with him. I feel somewhat aggrieved also because his remarks do a great disservice to leaders and members of the many active student organisations on the two campuses. I believe Mr Chiam himself recently paid a visit and gave a talk to a very lively audience in the University. If the honourable Member pays a visit to my Hall of residence, I am sure he, like many guests before him, will be quite amazed with the vibrancy and vigour in the Hall.

Mr Chiam See Tong: Is politics allowed?

Mr Ho Peng Kee: On the question of politics, Sir, I want to come back to my theme of balance. I think there is a place and a time for everything under heaven. One must certainly get one's priority right. When one is an undergraduate in the university, it is certainly not the time to be engaged in politics. I am sure many parents will agree with me. Politics, Sir, is something which is very intense. Politics drains you. I am sure, given the very tight constraints the students face in the university, they know their priorities, they know that in the university, it is the time to acquire academic knowledge and social skills, so that they can repay their debt which they owe to society later on as a working member of the population.

The other point I would like to just mention is that our universities have indeed turned out very fine minds, including that of Professor Tommy Koh, world-class in his chosen field of diplomacy, despite the illusory shackles that, Mr Chiam says, embrace our universities.

One last point is that this morning the Member for Bukit Gombak again raised a hollow cry that there are children who are qualified, but are deprived of places in independent schools. I think all of us know this assurance and the Government ---

Mr Ling How Doong: I did not say that. Please get your facts right.

Mr Ho Peng Kee: If I am wrong, I stand corrected. But in any case, I would like to remind this House ---

Mr Ling How Doong: Don't mislead this Parliament.

Mr Ho Peng Kee: --- that the Government has categorically said that no child shall be deprived of a place in an independent school if he is so qualified. That is the point we must bear in mind.

In any case, I am going to end, not with a Chinese idiom, which I think many Parliamentary colleagues have done, but I end with a quote, a quote from an American President whom all of us know, President John F Kennedy. This quote in its original form has been very well used, sometimes overused, but I think my adaptation is quite appropriate on an occasion like this. What I would like to say to all Singaporeans is this: do not just ask what the Government can do for you. I think that is a legitimate question. Do ask that question and you are right in asking that question, but also ask: what, as fellow Singaporeans, we can do for one another.

Finally, and very importantly, ask what we together as Singaporeans and individually as a Singaporean, we can do for Singapore.

With this, Sir, I support the motion.

Appendix B: THE NEE SOON EAST SONG

Nee Soon East Song
"For Community, For Residents"

1. It's time for fun and relaxation where would you like to be?
   Down to where there are friendly smiles
   Right here at Nee Soon East

2. Residents of our neighbourhood, working for a common good
   With a spirit of community
   Building a caring society

Chorus (English)

Right here, right now
That's where I want to be
Hand in hand, side by side
With my friends and family
Caring for each other
Looking out for one another
Right here at Nee Soon East
One heart, one home,
one community.

Chorus (Mandarin)

此时此地
就在这里
手牵手, 肩并肩
家人朋友在一起
彼此互相关怀
我们彼此互相照应
就在这 Nee Soon East

齐心共创
我们的选区

Chorus (Malay)

Sini, kini,
Aku mahu berada
Bersama, Bermesra
Dengan teman keluarga,
Kasih sesama
Pastikan kesejahteraan
Kini Nee Soon East
Hasrat, rumpun
Berkommuniti

Chorus (Tamil)

Ingum Yendrum
Idhuvae Yen Illam
Kaikorthu Tholserthu
Yendrum Nanbar Kudumbamai
Mattravar Nalanai Kaathida
Yendrum Anaivarai Paenida
Idhudhaan Nam Nee Soon East
Ullam Illam
Ondre Naam Enbom

Composed by Tonni and Jennifer Wei.

In launching the song at Nee Soon East's community centre on 10 October 1997, I said: "the motto and words of the song have been specially chosen to reflect our deepest desire for Nee Soon East. Our aspiration is to foster a community here where everyone will be proud to be a part of." To listen to the song, visit: https://www.facebook.com/nseyouths/videos/950543025037045/

Appendix C | **THE NEE SOON EAST TAGLINE**

We ♥ Nee Soon East

我们 ♥ 义顺东

Kami ♥ Nee Soon East

நாம் நீ சூன் கிழக்கை நேசிக்கிறோம் அல்லவா! ♥

Appendix D: A TRIBUTE FROM A KEY GRASSROOTS LEADER

Ho Peng Kee — a Journey of Passion

Prof Ho, our beloved Senior Minister of State
A legend from 1991
Every resident like a brother and sister
Children were like son and daughter.

The good Professor jogged and cycled
Saw and felt the pulse of NSE
Kind, considerate and caring
Pioneered our melodious Nee Soon East song

Dear Professor and Mentor
You served the community's rallying call
Holding the people's interests at the very core
You encouraged us to echo our love in this CC hall

Till today these lines echo
As the young now emulate "Prof's" steps
To this benevolent gentleman we owe
The bridging of the heartland's gaps

A trusted and honest team-mate
In his journey of passion to serve
After 20 years, he leaves behind
A gracious community to pass on
The torch of care and love

Thank you, dear Professor Ho Peng Kee
It has been a pleasure serving with thee
In our journey of service to the people of Nee Soon East!